Harvard Economic Studies

VOLUME 153

Awarded the David A. Wells Prize for 1978-79 and published from the income of the David A. Wells Fund.

The studies in this series are published under the direction of the Department of Economics of Harvard University. The department does not assume responsibility for the views expressed.

The Taxation
of Capital Income

ALAN J. AUERBACH

Harvard University Press

Cambridge, Massachusetts, and London, England
1983

10   9   8   7   6   5   4   3   2   1

Library of Congress Cataloging in Publication Data

Auerbach, Alan J.
    The taxation of capital income.

    (Harvard economic studies; v. 153)
    Includes index.
    1. Income tax—United States.   2. Corporations—
Taxation—United States.   3. Taxation—United States—
Effect of inflation on.   4. Capital levy—United States.
I. Title.   II. Series.
HJ4653.A3A93   1983   343.7305'245   83-122
ISBN 0-674-86845-5   347.3035245

For my parents

Contents

Preface

Each of the chapters of this book was written to stand on its own. In both the general introduction and in the introduction to the three parts of the book, however, I have tried to offer some additional perspective on the analysis presented in the chapters after a few years of hindsight and additional research into the problems of capital income taxation. Although some of my more recent written work develops ideas appearing in these early essays, it is omitted from the book in the interest of presenting a group of closely related chapters.

All of the chapters have previously been published and are reproduced here in their original versions. Chapter 1, "The Optimal Taxation of Heterogeneous Capital," and Chapter 5, "Wealth Maximization and the Cost of Capital," appeared in the *Quarterly Journal of Economics* (November 1979 and August 1979, respectively); I thank John Wiley and Sons for permission to reprint those articles. The *Journal of Public Economics* published "Tax Neutrality and the Social Discount Rate," Chapter 2, in April 1982, and "Share Valuation and Corporate Equity Policy," Chapter 4, in June 1979; I thank the North-Holland Publishing Company for reprint permission. "Efficient Design of Investment Incentives," Chapter 3, appeared as "A Note on the Efficient Design of Investment Incentives" in the *Economic Journal* in March 1981; Cambridge University Press kindly gave its permission to reprint the article here. Chapter 6, "Inflation and the Tax Treatment of Firm Behavior," appeared in the May 1981 issue of the *American Economic Review*; I thank the American Economic Association for reprint permission. "Inflation and the Choice of Asset Life," Chapter 7, appeared in the *Journal of Political Economy* in June 1979; I thank the University of Chicago Press for permission to reprint the article here.

My greatest intellectual debts incurred in the writing of this book are to Martin Feldstein and Jerry Green, first as thesis advisers, then as colleagues. Various collaborators have helped me gain a better understanding of the problems of capital income taxation. Among those in this category are Dale Jorgenson, Mervyn King, and Laurence Kotlikoff. Finally, many other colleagues, students, and friends have provided useful discussions, at times prompted by disagreements over the value of my ideas, but also serving to clarify them.

The Taxation of Capital Income

Introduction

The chapters that follow all deal with some aspect of capital income taxation. The nature of capital and its role in the production process have occupied the minds of economists since they were considered "moral philosophers," playing a particularly important role in the works of Marx, Wicksell, and many other classical economists, and in later times setting the occupants of one Cambridge against those of the other. The special attributes that make capital so distinct as a concept, and so controversial, have also influenced the more recent literature on the taxation of capital income.

Capital goods are durable; this has always presented a challenge for economists accustomed to analyzing problems using static, timeless models. From the "roundaboutness" of the Austrians to the "reswitching" controversy, there have been several views on what capital is, where it comes from, and what role capital income plays in the efficient allocation of resources over time. Because each capital good has a future, it is difficult to measure "the" capital stock in terms of the capital services provided today. It is similarly difficult to define capital income. These problems are particularly relevant to the study of capital income taxation, because the matter of efficiency is usually approached by examining the magnitude of the distortion a tax induces in the rate of return to capital.

Closely related to this discussion is the historical debate over the use of internal rate of return versus present value as the criterion in making investment decisions. In static models, both approaches prescribe the same simple formula for economic efficiency: choose the investment with the highest marginal product. The difficulty arises in determining the appropriate method when projects with different patterns of returns over time are compared. This problem of how to aggregate the stream of returns from a single project becomes particularly thorny when capital is taxed, for then the single discount rate to be used in present value calculations is replaced by at least two alternatives, the social rate of time preference and the social rate of return.

The issue of the choice of discount rate, common to the literature on public expenditure evaluation, has reemerged in the context of allocating investment incentives among capital goods with different service patterns.

Durability also lies behind the role of capital investment in aggregate fluctuations. Expectations about future events can exert a powerful force on investment today. How these expectations are formed is still subject to some debate, but the notion lingers that the "animal spirits" envisioned by Keynes are still at work. The very idea of an "investment incentive" suggests not a long-run policy for capital income taxation, but rather a temporary palliative aimed at counteracting the instability of aggregate investment.

Also because of its durability, capital serves as a store of value. Hence capital and its ownership have always been related to questions of income distribution. A full treatment of what the "optimal" level of capital income taxation is ought to include not only an efficiency calculation, but also a consideration of intra- and intergenerational equity.

The way capital is owned as well as how it is distributed also influences how capital is taxed. In the United States, as in most other industrialized countries, most business capital is held indirectly by households in the form of financial claims issued by corporations. These corporations exist as separate legal entities, and are taxed as such. The coordination of the goals of corporate managers and those of stockholders and bondholders is influenced by the coexistence of corporate and personal tax systems. Because these two systems are not "integrated" to work in concert, anomalous and unforeseen influences can be exerted on corporate financial and investment decisions by changes in tax policy.

The fact that capital plays a role in productivity growth perhaps accounts for the fact that capital income taxation has received so much attention recently. The well-documented decline in U.S. productivity growth experienced during the 1970s may have been related in a number of ways to the concurrent pattern of capital accumulation. It is particularly disturbing to some that taxes on capital income in the 1970s may have reduced both capital formation in general and the risk-taking associated with investment in innovation. Inflation plays an insidious role here, for the difficulty in measuring capital income becomes even more acute when changes in the price level must be taken into account. Unfortunately, the U.S. tax system is ill-equipped to make such corrections.

The seven chapters that follow are divided into three sections. The

first section considers the efficiency of capital income taxation. Two important questions are, first, how heavily capital income should be taxed, and, second, for a given level of capital income taxation, how the tax burden should be distributed over different kinds of capital. The two chapters in the second section deal specifically with the interaction of corporate and personal tax systems such as those in the United States, where interest payments by corporations are tax deductible but dividends are not, and capital gains are taxed at rates substantially below those on ordinary income. The final two chapters focus on the impact of inflation on the allocation of capital and the incentive to invest in the context of the U.S. tax system.

It is difficult to say what the important issues in capital income taxation will be during the next several years. During the 1970s, there were three questions, corresponding roughly to the three sections of this book, that received a great deal of attention in the literature on capital income taxation: whether consumption was a better tax base than income, how corporate and personal income taxes could be coordinated through integration, and how the tax system could be adapted to deal with inflation.

The passage by Congress of the Economic Recovery Tax Act of 1981 has settled, or at least changed, each of these questions. Under the provisions of the Accelerated Cost Recovery System, particularly the rapid tax writeoff of depreciable business assets, the revenues from the corporate income tax have been greatly reduced, and the question of integration has been replaced by one of how to phase out the corporate tax structure. Even with very small revenues in the aggregate, the corporate tax in its current form may exert strong effects on the level and allocation of investment, by offering a subsidy to the income generated by some kinds of new investment and financing this subsidy with taxes on other sources of investment and non-investment income. (See the discussion in Auerbach, "The New Economics of Accelerated Depreciation," *Boston College Law Review* 23 [September 1982], 1327-1355.)

The income-consumption debate may have been brought to an end by the general reduction in capital income taxes resulting from ACRS as well as other parts of the new tax law that extend full or partial exclusion from the income tax to a greater proportion of individual capital income. Here, too, future discussion may be about how this transition should be completed. An example is the problem posed by the continued availability of interest deductibility when certain forms of interest income are tax exempt.

The inflation issue, like the other two, has been settled in one sense

but not another. Effective tax rates have been reduced but still depend on the inflation rate. Part of the potential benefit of moving to a consumption tax would be that it no longer would be necessary to distinguish real from nominal income: income would no longer be taxed. We have yet to achieve this simplification, because our current tax system resembles a consumption tax only in that much of capital income faces a light tax burden, on average. This low tax has been achieved by very complicated and indirect means that do not seem very rational, given their full effect.

The timing of the new tax law suggests that its formulation may have resulted, in part, from a growing appreciation of the effects of the old tax law on capital formation and allocation. But the chosen methods of dealing with shortcomings in the old tax law have raised new problems themselves. Perhaps we have passed through an era in which the important problems of capital taxation have been recognized, and it is now time to deal carefully with the solutions we have imposed.

PART I

OPTIMAL CAPITAL TAXATION AND INVESTMENT INCENTIVES

The first chapter in Part I, "The Optimal Taxation of Heterogeneous Capital," asks how high tax rates on capital income should be, and when rates on different kinds of capital income should differ.

The answer to the first question depends on what the government's objective is. In this chapter I consider a growth model with overlapping generations in which no bequests occur, and derive those taxes that maximize the utility of a representative individual in the economy's long-run steady state. In such a framework an externality exists in that even without distortionary taxes, steady-state utility is below its highest feasible level: the economy is not on its "Golden Rule" growth path. As a result, optimal taxes on capital and labor result as a compromise between minimizing the excess burden of taxation and correcting this externality. It is important to remember that this outcome is dependent on what the government seeks to maximize. In achieving a higher steady-state utility level, the optimal tax policy may reduce the welfare of generations alive during the transition to the steady state. Unfortunately, it is difficult to examine such transitions analytically. (A perfect foresight simulation model is applied to this question in Auerbach et al., "The Efficiency Gains from Dynamic Tax Reform," *International Economic Review*, forthcoming.)

Whether capital income taxes, whatever their level, should be equal depends on the state of taxes in the rest of the economy. In the model developed in the first chapter, income from different kinds of capital should be taxed at different rates unless labor income is taxed optimally or labor is of equal complementarity in production to different types of capital. This result is particularly relevant to the process of designing investment incentives. However, its interpretation is complicated by the fact that the U.S. tax system, unlike the model of Chapter 1, does not actually impose a pure income tax on capital income.

To understand the nature of this problem, it is helpful to think of the income from an asset over a period of time as consisting of two parts: the tangible return plus the change in the asset's value. If the asset is a share of stock, for example, the two sources of income are dividends and capital gains. For a capital good such as a plant or a machine, the tangible component of income is the quasi-rent it earns, and the change in value (customarily assumed to be negative) is depreciation. The definition of depreciation as the reduction in an

5

asset's value, formulated by Hotelling in 1925, is only one of several definitions; it is also common practice to refer to the decline in the productivity of a capital good as depreciation. These two definitions will normally coincide only if asset productivity decreases exponentially over time at a constant rate, in which case asset value declines at the same rate. In general, the rate of change in an asset's value will depend not only on its concurrent productivity decline, but, also on the pattern of future quasi-rents. Because the term depreciation can have more than one meaning, it is customary to refer to Hotelling's definition as "economic" depreciation.

A third view of depreciation is the schedule of income tax deductions the owner of an asset receives after its purchase. If such deductions were patterned on economic depreciation, then an income tax with a base corresponding to the Haig-Simons income concept of cash flow plus accretions to wealth would result. Each component of income, quasi-rents and depreciation, would be taxed at the same rate at each point in the asset's life, so there would be no ambiguity about the tax rate on the asset's income. It is difficult, however, to measure economic depreciation exactly; and, perhaps more relevant, the acceleration of depreciation allowances has commonly been used to stimulate investment. For both reasons, depreciation allowances are often markedly different from economic depreciation. As a result, the income from an investment good faces a different tax rate in each year: higher than the statutory rate when allowances are less than economic depreciation, and lower when allowances are higher or when there is an investment tax credit received. Unless tax depreciation and economic depreciation are identical, an aggregation problem confronts the calculation of average or "effective" tax rates that are appropriate for applying the results of Chapter 1.

The solution to this problem is discussed in Chapter 2, "Tax Neutrality and the Social Discount Rate." The analysis suggests that the effective tax rate on an asset's income stream should be calculated as the hypothetical tax rate on economic income to which the investor facing the actual tax schedule would be indifferent. An equivalent definition of this measure is the ratio of the difference between the internal rates of return of the project's gross-of-tax and net-of-tax cash flows to the internal rate of return of gross flows.

In calculating the effective tax rate on investment, the way the investment is financed may be relevant. The tax treatment of debt and equity differ, as discussed in detail in the next section of this book. However, a particular question, examined in "Efficient Design of Investment Incentives," is related to the issues just discussed: how might the tax system affect the amount of borrowing an investor can do? If the loan is secured, it may be limited by the value of the invest-

ment project. This value, at any time, depends on the project's future stream of after-tax returns, and hence on the tax system itself. Likewise, economic depreciation, representing the change in this value over time, also depends on the actual tax system in force.

There is one additional point, not discussed thus far, that deserves some mention. While investment is often associated with risk-taking, this relationship is ignored here. As discussed in Auerbach, "Evaluating the Taxation of Risky Assets," Harvard Institute of Economic Research Discussion Paper No. 857 (November 1981), one can calculate meaningful effective tax rates for risky assets by adjusting each project's gross-of-tax and net-of-tax returns for risk and then computing the effective tax rate, as before. Such a procedure yields a different result than one based on expected returns. The two measures may differ quite substantially.

The chapters in Part I also ignore the existence of separate personal and corporate tax structures and inflation. The effects of adding these factors are explored in Parts II and III.

1

The Optimal Taxation of Heterogeneous Capital

I. INTRODUCTION

The creation of new capital through individual savings decisions has long been considered an important economic issue. An aspect that has been discussed frequently, from both positive and normative viewpoints, is the influence of taxation on capital formation.

One point that is commonly made is that the introduction of a differential tax on capital income from different sources is deleterious to social welfare because it induces inefficiency in production arising out of a misallocation of capital. Harberger [1966] has, perhaps, presented the best known formulation of this argument in reference to the U. S. corporate income tax. On a related subject, one finds the literature on investment incentives punctuated by the advocacy of "neutrality," which by some definitions corresponds to the maintenance of equal effective rates of tax on different investments.[1]

Again using static welfare analysis, Harberger [1964] finds that the introduction of a tax on capital income induces a welfare loss, the magnitude of which depends on the responsiveness of savings to changes in the rate of taxation, and which is zero if savings, and hence capital supply, are inelastic. Feldstein [1978] has criticized this approach, arguing that the distortions relevant in measuring the welfare effects of taxation are those in consumption behavior, and that savings is of interest only insofar as it relates to future consumption. Feldstein analyzed the problem using a framework suggested by Atkinson and Stiglitz [1976], in which capital and labor income taxes are assessed on an individual who lives for two periods, works only in the first and saves for consumption in the second. One main conclusion of this

The author has benefited from several discussions with Martin Feldstein and Jerry Green, as well as comments received during various presentations of earlier drafts.

1. See Auerbach [1978] for a discussion of this issue.

approach is that it is the elasticity of demand for second-period consumption, and not the supply elasticity of savings, which determines the welfare loss from capital income taxation. A second result, drawn from static optimal tax theory, is that, if revenue must be raised by the government, capital income should be taxed only if leisure is a relative complement to either first-period or second-period consumption.[2] In particular, it will never be optimal to tax capital income if utility may be expressed as a function weakly separable into leisure and consumption, and preferences are homothetic with respect to consumption goods (see Sandmo, 1974).

The results presented in this paper call into question the general validity of the conclusions outlined above. We find that there are important elements of the problem of the optimal taxation of income from heterogeneous capital that are not captured by such static approaches.

II. THE MODEL

We build on the neoclassical growth model introduced by Diamond [1965], considering an economy with one production sector and overlapping generations of individuals who live for two periods. These generations grow in size at a rate n, so that the population sizes of the older generations at times t and s are related by

(1) $$N_t/N_s = (1 + n)^{t-s}.$$

Individuals work only in the first period, choosing to supply a quantity L of labor out of an endowment $\bar{L}$. We denote as $\tilde{L}$ the corresponding consumption of leisure, $\bar{L} - L$. Out of first period wages, workers consume a level C_1, saving the rest that, along with its return, is used to consume C_2 in the second period. We initially assume there to be no bequests, although we shall return to this issue later. Individual preferences are identical, and may be described by the utility function,

(2) $$U = U(C_1, C_2, \tilde{L}).$$

The gross output in the economy is produced using three inputs, labor and the services from two distinct types of capital good, denoted

---

2. The relative degree of complementarity between the two kinds of consumption and leisure is assessed by comparing the compensated elasticities of the demand for each with respect to the price of leisure.

type 1 and type 2. Both types of capital are created from the same homogeneous output, but once investment occurs, it is irreversible. The level of capital services yielded by a unit of capital of type i and age j is represented by the term A_{ij}. We normalize the vectors $\mathbf{A}_1$ and $\mathbf{A}_2$ so that new investment goods of each type yield one unit of capital services; that is, $A_{11} = A_{21} = 1$. If we let I_{is} represent the gross investment in capital of type i that occurs during period s, then the total level of capital services, or the capital stock, of type i available for production during period t is

$$(3) \qquad K_{it} = \sum_{s=-\infty}^{t-1} A_{it-s} I_{is}.$$

The production technology obeys constant returns to scale in its three inputs, and may be represented by the function,

$$(4) \qquad G_t = H(K_{1t}, K_{2t}, L_t) \qquad H_i > 0; \qquad H_{ii} < 0,$$

where L_t is the total labor supply in period t. The function H is unchanging over time; there is no technical change.

We assume that government must raise a certain level of revenue R_t in each period t, and that this amount grows in fixed proportion to the population. We limit the scope of our analysis to the examination of the characteristics of the economy in a steady state of balanced growth,[3] and consider, under various assumptions concerning the instruments available to government, the nature of the balanced growth path on which per capita utility is maximized. This would be the relevant steady state if government desired to maximize a social welfare function consisting of an unweighted sum of per capita levels of utility attained by future generations, such as

$$(5) \qquad W_t = \sum_{s=t}^{T} U_s,$$

where U_s is per capita utility of generation s and T is some distant terminal time.[4] Because the population grows at rate n, the use of such a criterion would be equivalent to discounting the simple sum of in-

---

3. There is a question, raised by Hahn [1966], of whether an economy with heterogeneous capital goods, like the one described above, would actually converge to a balanced growth path under competitive market conditions. Shell and Stiglitz [1967] have explored this issue and discussed various properties that would contribute to stability.

4. Roughly speaking, if T is finite but sufficiently large, the balanced growth path on which individual utility is maximized is a "turnpike" near which the optimal path remains for an arbitrarily large portion of the time. See Intriligator [1971] for a discussion.

dividual utilities in each generation at rate $(1 + n)$.[5] This choice of n as the discount rate is arbitrary, and the results could be modified to reflect the addition of a pure rate of time discount δ resulting in a discount rate of $n + \delta$.[6] This would remove the problem that would ensue in (5) if T were infinite but would add great complexity to many of the calculations that follow.

III. THE CONTROLLED ECONOMY

To aid in the interpretation of the results that occur when there is competitive behavior and taxation, we consider first the optimum that would be chosen by a planner who could select levels of production and consumption from the set of feasible alternatives.

Consumption in each period equals

(6) $\qquad C_t = C_1 N_{t+1} + C_2 N_t = [C_1(1 + n) + C_2]N_t.$

Output in each period is exhausted by consumption, capital investment, and revenue. In any steady state, investment in each type of capital grows at rate n, so that (3) yields

(7) $\qquad K_{it} = I_{it} \sum_{s=-\infty}^{t-1} A_{it-s}(1 + n)^{-(t-s)}.$

If we define $R = R_t/N_t$, $K_i = K_{it}/N_t$, and $I_i = I_{it}/N_t$ as revenue, capital, and investment per older generation member, and let

(8) $\qquad A_i(n) = \sum_{s=1}^{\infty} (1 + n)^{-s}A_{is}$

be the present value of services received from a unit of new capital, discounted at rate n, then the constraint subject to which steady-state utility is to be maximized becomes

(9) $\quad C_1(1 + n) + C_2 + R + I_1 + I_2 = H[A_1(n)I_1, A_2(n)I_2, (1 + n)L].$

The first-order conditions yield

(10.1) $\qquad \dfrac{U_2}{U_1} = \dfrac{1}{1 + n}$

5. That is, (5) may be rewritten as
$$W_t = N_t^{-1} \sum_{s=t}^{T} (1 + n)^{-(s-t)}(N_s u_s).$$

6. The use of a pure rate of discount in related contexts may be found in Arrow and Kurz [1970], Diamond [1973], and Pestieau [1974].

(10.2)
$$\frac{U_3}{U_1} = H_3$$

(10.3)　　　　$H_i A_i(n) = 1$　　$(i = 1,2).$

Condition (10.1) says that the individual rate of time preference should equal the government discount rate, which is the rate of population growth. (10.2) calls for the equation of the marginal product of labor with the marginal disutility incurred in its supply. (10.3) calls for investment to occur in each type of capital until the present value of such investments, discounted at the social discount rate, is zero.[7]

IV. COMPETITIVE BEHAVIOR

In this regime individuals receive a net wage rate w for labor supplied in the first period and may save for second-period consumption through the purchase of capital or one-period bonds issued by the government. Since there is no uncertainty in this model, these alternative investments must yield the same net rate of return, which we denote by r. Consumers maximize utility subject to the budget constraint,

(11)　　　　$C_2 = (1 + r)(wL - C_1) = (1 + r)S,$

where S is per capita savings. From utility maximization we may derive the indirect utility function:

(12)　　　　　　$V = V(w,r).$

It may be shown that

(13)　　　　$V_w = \lambda(1 + r)L; \quad V_r = \lambda S,$

where λ is the marginal utility of labor endowment measured in units of second-period consumption. We may also represent the factor supply functions:

(14)　　　　$S^s = S^s(w,r); \quad L^s = L^s(w,r).$

Consumer theory alone does not allow us to determine the sign of any of the supply derivatives.

We assume that government raises its required revenue through

---

7. Condition (10.3) corresponds to the "Neo-Classical Theorem" of Robinson [1962]. For the case in which capital of type i is homogeneous and nondepreciating, $A_{ij} = 1$ for all j, which implies that $A_i(n) = 1/n$. Thus, (10.3) yields the "Golden Rule" of Phelps [1961], specifying that the marginal product of capital H_i should equal n.

taxes on labor income and capital income and the issuance of debt. The tax schedule may vary with the type of capital, with Z_{ij} being the tax assessed per unit of capital good of type i and age j (in its jth period of service).

For the purposes of our analysis, it is easiest to visualize individuals as investing in capital goods directly and renting them to firms, rather than buying the firms directly. Since constant returns to scale and perfect competition together guarantee zero profits at the firm level, the two approaches lead to the same results. For equilibrium in the capital market to hold, the net rate of return on all capital assets must equal r. The return is composed of the rental income, net of tax, plus any capital gain realized upon sale. Perfect competition ensures that each unit of capital will receive its marginal product, which is $H_i A_{ij}$ for a unit of type i and age j. Thus, letting q_{ij} be the beginning-of-period market value of such a good, we have

$$(15) \qquad rq_{ij} = (q_{ij+1} - q_{ij}) + H_i A_{ij} - Z_{ij} \quad (i = 1,2).$$

When an asset declines in value over time, this decline, which is minus the capital gain, is referred to as the "economic depreciation" of the asset.[8]

According to the current U. S. corporate tax structure, physical rents from capital are taxed at a constant rate, after the allowance of a deduction for depreciation. Letting τ_i be the tax rate on income from capital of type i, and D_{ij} the deduction allowed for a unit of type i and age j, this means that

$$(16) \qquad Z_{ij} = \tau_i (H_i A_{ij} - D_{ij}) \quad (i = 1,2).$$

It is clear that if D_{ij} exceeds true economic depreciation, which equals $-(q_{ij+1} - q_{ij})$, then the effective tax rate is less than τ_i. Similarly, if D_{ij} is less than economic depreciation, then the effective tax rate is greater than τ_i. In the special case in which D_{ij} always corresponds to economic depreciation, the effective tax rate is always τ_i.[9]

It is highly unlikely that depreciation schedules actually in use resemble economic depreciation. Various acceleration schemes provide for a speeding up of allowances, with D_{ij} being greater than economic depreciation for small j and smaller for large j. In the presence of inflation, the non-indexed allowances decline in value. Thus, even if the schedule were correct in the absence of inflation, the

8. Since there is no inflation in this model, the change in q represents a real change in value.
9. This property of economic depreciation deductions was first discussed by Samuelson [1964].

real values of D_{ij} become smaller and smaller relative to real depreciation as j increases.[10]

For the purposes of the present analysis, we assume that the tax schedules for both types of capital reflect economic depreciation. Letting

$$(17) \qquad t_i = \frac{r}{1 - \tau_i} - r \qquad (i = 1,2)$$

be the unit tax corresponding to the ad valorem tax τ_i, we get

$$(18) \qquad \bar{Z}_{ij} = t_i q_{ij} \quad (i = 1,2).$$

Equations (15), (16), and (18) are combined to form the difference equation,

$$(19) \qquad q_{ij+1} = (1 + r + t_i)q_{ij} - H_i A_{ij} \quad (i = 1,2),$$

which, assuming that q_{ij} is finite as j approaches infinity, may be solved to obtain the valuation formula,

$$(20) \qquad q_{ij} = \sum_{k=j}^{\infty} (1 + r + t_i)^{-(k-j+1)} H_i A_{ik} \quad (i = 1,2).$$

In equilibrium the market value of a new capital good of either type must equal its price, which is unity, since both types of good come from the same homogeneous output:

$$(21) \qquad q_{i1} = 1 \quad (i = 1,2).$$

Thus, we may view the investment process as one in which new investments in capital of type i are accepted until the present value, when discounted at the rate $r + t_i$ (see equation (20)), equals zero. We define the average value of the type i capital stock at time t, which is constant in a steady state, by

$$(22) \qquad q_i = \frac{\sum_{j=1}^{\infty} q_{ij} I_{it-j}}{K_{it}} \quad (i = 1,2).$$

The total tax revenue collected from type i capital at the end of period t is

$$(23) \qquad T_{it} = \sum_{j=1}^{\infty} \bar{Z}_{ij} I_{it-j} \quad (i = 1,2),$$

which, by (18) and (22), yields

10. See Auerbach [1979] for an analysis of the impact of the failure to index depreciation allowances.

(24) $$T_{it} = t_i q_i K_{it} \quad (i = 1,2).$$

From the assumption of competitive firm behavior, it follows that firms will equate the marginal product of labor with the gross wage:

(25) $$H_3 = w + t_w,$$

where t_w is the unit tax on labor services.[11]

In the steady state, the size of the government debt grows at rate n. The net revenue in each period is new sales less interest payments on existing debt. If we let B_t be the amount of debt outstanding during period t, this revenue equals $(n - r)B_t$. Thus, the government's revenue constraint in period t is

(26) $$R_t = t_1 q_1 K_{1t} + t_2 q_2 K_{2t} + t_w L_t + (n - r)B_t.$$

Dividing both sides of (26) by N_t, and letting $x_i = t_i q_i$ be the tax per unit of capital of type i, we see that (26) becomes

(27) $$R = x_1 K_1 + x_2 K_2 + t_w (1 + n)L + (n - r)B,$$

where $B = B_t/N_t$.

Since individual savings is exhausted by purchases of debt and equity, it follows that

(28) $$S = B + q_1 K_1 + q_1 K_2.$$

V. OPTIMAL FACTOR TAXATION

What are the characteristics of the optimal taxes called for when government is free to set the values of t_1, t_2, t_w, and, perhaps, the level of debt as well? In a static context Diamond and Mirrlees [1971] have found that, if all transactions between the household and production sector may be taxed, it will not be generally optimal to make use of additional tax instruments that distort allocation within the production sector. An analogy to the present case might be drawn to suggest that the required rates of return on projects of type 1 and type 2, $r + t_1$ and $r + t_2$, should be equal, which implies a uniform tax on capital income. We shall see below under what conditions such an analogy is appropriate.

The object here is to maximize utility, as represented in (12), subject to the revenue constraint (27) by varying the taxes t_w, t_1, and

---

11. Note that, for the case of nondepreciating capital ($A_{ij} \equiv 1$), (20) reduces to a similar condition, that $H_i = r + t_i$.

t_2 and the level of bonds outstanding per capita B. It turns out to be easier to express the taxes as functions of the variables K_1, K_2, and L, and derive first-order conditions with respect to these variables, than it is to differentiate with respect to the taxes themselves.

The first-order conditions necessary for an optimum are

$$(29.1) \qquad \lambda \left[S \frac{dr}{dK_i} + (1+r)L \frac{dw}{dK_i} \right]$$

$$+ \mu \left[x_i + K_1 \frac{dx_1}{dK_i} + K_2 \frac{dx_2}{dK_i} + (1+n)L \frac{dt_w}{dK_i} - B \frac{dr}{dK_i} \right] = 0$$

$$(i = 1,2)$$

$$(29.2) \qquad \lambda \left[S \frac{dr}{dL} + (1+r)L \frac{dw}{dL} \right]$$

$$+ \mu \left[t_w(1+n) + K_1 \frac{dx_1}{dL} + K_2 \frac{dx_2}{dL} + (1+n)L \frac{dt_w}{dL} - B \frac{dr}{dL} \right] = 0$$

$$(29.3) \qquad \lambda \left[S \frac{dr}{dB} + (1+r)L \frac{dw}{dB} \right]$$

$$+ \mu \left[(n-r) + K_1 \frac{dx_1}{dB} + K_2 \frac{dx_2}{dB} + (1+n)L \frac{dt_w}{dB} - B \frac{dr}{dB} \right] = 0,$$

where μ is the Lagrange multiplier of the revenue constraint. If bonds are not present as an instrument, then condition (29.3) is dropped and B set equal to zero.

The derivative of a term y with respect to any parameter θ may be expressed as

$$(30) \qquad \frac{dy}{d\theta} = \frac{\partial y}{\partial r} \cdot \frac{dr}{d\theta} + \frac{\partial y}{\partial w} \cdot \frac{dw}{d\theta} + \frac{d\hat{y}}{d\theta},$$

where $d\hat{y}/d\theta$ is the derivative of y with respect to θ, holding r and w fixed. Using (30) and (25), we may rewrite conditions (29) as

$$(31.1) \qquad \lambda \left[S \frac{dr}{dK_i} + (1+r)L \frac{dw}{dK_i} \right]$$

$$+ \mu \left[x_i + K_1 \frac{d\hat{x}_1}{dK_i} + K_2 \frac{d\hat{x}_2}{dK_i} + (1+n)LH_{3i} + P_r \frac{dr}{dK_i} + P_w \frac{dw}{dK_i} \right]$$

$$= 0 \quad (i = 1,2)$$

(31.2) $\lambda \left[S \dfrac{dr}{dL} + (1 + r)L \dfrac{dw}{dL} \right]$

$$+ \mu \left[t_w (1 + n) + K_1 \dfrac{d\hat{x}_1}{dL} + K_2 \dfrac{d\hat{x}_2}{dL} \right.$$

$$\left. + (1 + n)LH_{33} + P_r \dfrac{dr}{dL} + P_w \dfrac{dw}{dL} \right] = 0$$

(31.3) $\lambda \left[S \dfrac{dr}{dB} + (1 + r)L \dfrac{dw}{dB} \right]$

$$+ \mu \left[(n - r) + K_1 \dfrac{d\hat{x}_1}{dB} + K_2 \dfrac{d\hat{x}_2}{dB} + P_r \dfrac{dr}{dB} + P_w \dfrac{dw}{dB} \right] = 0,$$

where P_r and P_w are defined by

(32) $$P_r = K_1 \dfrac{\partial x_1}{\partial r} + K_2 \dfrac{\partial x_2}{\partial r} - B$$

$$P_w = K_1 \dfrac{\partial x_1}{\partial w} + K_2 \dfrac{\partial x_2}{\partial w} - (1 + n)L.$$

We may solve for the derivatives of r and w with respect to K_1, K_2, L, and B by using the supply functions (14) in conjunction with equation (28). A change in $K_1(K_2)$, holding $K_2(K_1)$, L, and B constant, must affect r and w in such a way that $S(w,r)$ and $(q_1 K_1 + q_2 K_2 + B)$ change by the identical amount, and there is no change in $L(w,r)$. A change in L, holding K_1, K_2, and B constant, must cause an equal change in $L(w,r)$, and identical changes in $(q_1 K_1 + q_2 K_2 + B)$ and $S(w,r)$. Finally, a change in B, holding K_1, K_2, and L fixed, must cause identical changes in $(q_1 K_1 + q_2 K_2 + B)$ and $S(w,r)$, and no change in $L(w,r)$. Solving for the various derivatives, we obtain

(33.1) $$\dfrac{dr}{dK_i} = \dfrac{M_i L_w}{\Delta}; \quad \dfrac{dw}{dK_i} = \dfrac{-M_i L_r}{\Delta} \quad (i = 1,2)$$

(33.2) $$\dfrac{dr}{dB} = \dfrac{M_B L_w}{\Delta}; \quad \dfrac{dw}{dB} = \dfrac{-M_B L_r}{\Delta}$$

(33.3) $$\dfrac{dr}{dL} = \dfrac{[M_L L_w - (S_w + Q_w)]}{\Delta}$$

$$\dfrac{dw}{dL} = \dfrac{-[M_L L_r - (S_r + Q_r)]}{\Delta},$$

where

$$(34.1) \qquad M_i = q_i + K_1 \frac{d\hat{q}_1}{dK_i} + K_2 \frac{d\hat{q}_2}{dK_i} \quad (i = 1,2)$$

$$(34.2) \qquad M_B = 1 + K_1 \frac{d\hat{q}_1}{dB} + K_2 \frac{d\hat{q}_2}{dB}$$

$$(34.3) \qquad M_L = K_1 \frac{d\hat{q}_1}{dL} + K_2 \frac{d\hat{q}_2}{dL}$$

$$(34.4) \qquad \Delta = (S_r + Q_r)L_w - (S_w + Q_w)L_r$$

and Q_r and Q_w are defined by

$$(35) \qquad Q_r = K_1 \frac{\partial q_1}{\partial r} + K_2 \frac{\partial q_2}{\partial r}$$

$$Q_w = K_1 \frac{\partial q_1}{\partial w} + K_2 \frac{\partial q_2}{\partial w}.$$

Substituting (33.1) into (31.1), we obtain

$$(36) \quad \lambda \left[S \frac{L_w}{\Delta} - (1 + r)L \frac{L_r}{\Delta} \right] + \mu \left[R_i + P_r \frac{L_w}{\Delta} - P_w \frac{L_r}{\Delta} \right] = 0$$

$$(i = 1,2),$$

where

$$(37) \qquad R_i = \left[x_i + K_1 \frac{d\hat{x}_1}{dK_i} + K_2 \frac{d\hat{x}_2}{dK_i} + (1 + n)LH_{3i} \right] \Big/ M_i$$

$$(i = 1,2).$$

Note that (36) is valid whether or not bonds exist in the model. It is clear that $R_1 = R_2$.

We now consider the circumstances under which it is optimal for the taxes on the two types of capital, t_1 and t_2, to be set equal.

A. No Depreciation

If each type of capital good yields a constant stream of services over an infinite lifetime, then $A_{ij} = 1$ for $i = 1,2$ and positive j. From (20) it follows that q_{ij} is independent of j. By (21) this means that $q_{ij} \equiv 1$. It then follows from (3) and (22) that $q_1 = q_2 = 1$. Equation (20) implies that $t_i = H_i - r$. Given the fact that $x_i = t_i q_i$, we may use this information to simplify expression (37), obtaining

$$(38) \quad R_i = t_i + [K_1 H_{1i} + K_2 H_{2i} + (1 + n)LH_{3i}] \quad (i = 1,2).$$

It is a simple consequence of Euler's Theorem that the term in

brackets is zero. Thus, $R_1 = t_1$, and $R_2 = t_2$. It follows that $t_1 = t_2$.

B. Exponential Depreciation

A more general case is that in which each type of capital does decay, but at a constant rate; that is, for all $j \geq 1$:

$$(39) \qquad\qquad A_{ij} = (1 - \delta_i)^{(j-1)} \qquad (i = 1,2),$$

where δ_i is the decay rate of type i capital. Substituting (39) into (20), we find that $q_{ij} = (1 - \delta_i)^{(j-1)}q_{i1}$. By (21) and (39) this implies that $q_{ij} = A_{ij}$. If we substitute A_{ij} for q_{ij} in (22), it follows from a comparison with (3) that $q_1 = q_2 = 1$. Equation (20) implies that $t_i = H_i - r - \delta_i$. Since δ_1 and δ_2 are fixed, (37) once again reduces to (38), and $t_1 = t_2$.

C. General Depreciation

In the two previous cases we found it optimal to tax capital income uniformly, independent of whether debt was also available as an instrument. However, such a result does not obtain in the general case.

Using the definition that $x_i = t_i q_i$, we may rewrite (37) as

$$(40) \quad R_i = t_i + \left[K_1 \left(q_1 \frac{d\hat{t}_1}{dK_i} - H_{1i} \right) + K_2 \left(q_2 \frac{d\hat{t}_2}{dK_i} - H_{2i} \right) \right] \bigg/ M_i$$

$$(i = 1,2).$$

Since $R_1 = R_2$, the taxes t_1 and t_2 will not be equal unless the second term on the right-hand side of (40) is independent of i. We shall not demonstrate so explicitly, but it is easy to see from the examination of particular examples that this is unlikely in the absence of debt.

Now, suppose that the debt instrument is available to the government planner. Then the first-order condition (31.3) applies. Substituting in equations (33.2), we obtain

$$(41) \quad \lambda \left[S \frac{L_w}{\Delta} - (1 + r)L \frac{L_r}{\Delta} \right] + \mu \left[R_B + P_r \frac{L_w}{\Delta} - P_w \frac{L_r}{\Delta} \right] = 0,$$

where

$$(42) \qquad R_B = \left[(n - r) + K_1 \frac{d\hat{x}_1}{dB} + K_2 \frac{d\hat{x}_2}{dB} \right] \bigg/ M_B.$$

It is evident from comparing (36) and (41) that $R_B = R_1 = R_2$.

Equation (42) may be simplified. For $j = 1$, we substitute (21) into (20) to obtain

(43) $$1 = \sum_{k=1}^{\infty} (1 + r + t_i)^{-k} H_i A_{ik} \quad (i = 1,2)$$

from which it follows that $dt_i/dB = 0.$[12] Combining (7), (20), and (22), we obtain an expression for q_i:

(44) $$q_i = \left[\sum_{k=1}^{\infty} (1 + n)^{-k} A_{ik} \right]^{-1}$$

$$\times \sum_{k=1}^{\infty} (1 + n)^{-k} \sum_{j=k}^{\infty} (1 + r + t_i)^{-(j-k+1)} H_i A_{ij} \quad (i = 1,2).$$

Since $dt_i/dB = 0$, it follows from (44) that $dq_i/dB = 0$. These two results together imply that (42) reduces to

(45) $$R_B = n - r.$$

As long as the optimal values of t_1 and t_2 are the only ones for which the requirement that $R_1 = R_2 = R_B$ is satisfied, then we can demonstrate that these taxes satisfy

(46) $$t_1 = t_2 = n - r,$$

which means that the discount rates implicit in project evaluation, $r + t_1$ and $r + t_2$, are not only the same, but are also equal to the government discount rate n.[13] This result is now demonstrated. Suppose that (46) holds. Then (44) yields

(47) $$q_i = \left[\sum_{k=1}^{\infty} (1 + r + t_i)^{-k} A_{ik} \right]^{-1}$$

$$\times \sum_{k=1}^{\infty} k(1 + r + t_i)^{-(k+1)} H_i A_{ik} \quad (i = 1,2),$$

which, by (43), yields

(48) $$q_i = H_i^2 \sum_{k=1}^{\infty} k(1 + r + t_i)^{-(k+1)} A_{ik} \quad (i = 1,2).$$

Differentiating (43) with respect to K_j, holding r and w fixed, we obtain

---

12. This is true since K_1, K_2, and L are held fixed and, by construction, $dr/dB = 0$.

13. In the case in which capital does not depreciate, (46) implies that the marginal product of capital of each type equals n, which is similar to results derived by Diamond [1973] and Pestieau [1974] for models with one type of private capital.

(49) $H_{ij} = H_i^2 \sum_{k=1}^{\infty} k(1 + r + t_i)^{-(k+1)} A_{ik} \dfrac{d\hat{t}_i}{dK_j}$ $(i,j = 1,2)$.

Combination of (48) and (49) yields

(50) $H_{ij} = q_i \dfrac{d\hat{t}_i}{dK_j}$ $(i,j = 1,2)$.

Substituting (50) into (40) yields the required result, that $R_1 = R_2 = n - r$.

The results of this section indicate that it will generally be optimal to set equal taxes on the different types of capital only if the resulting uniform discount rate, $r + t_1 = r + t_2$, equals the social discount rate, which in our example is the population growth rate n, and that government debt may be used to ensure such an outcome. Only when services from capital goods are either constant or declining at a constant positive rate will uniform taxes on capital be generally optimal. A related result which can be demonstrated is that this special property of capital with exponential decay is dependent on the assumption that depreciation allowances correspond to economic depreciation.

VI. THE NATURE OF OPTIMAL TAXES

To understand how our results relate to previous work, we consider the special case in which capital goods of each type are homogeneous, providing constant services over infinite lifetimes. In this case we found in the previous section that $q_1 = q_2 = 1$. From inspection of equations (34) and (35), it follows that $M_1 = M_2 = M_B = 1$, $M_L = Q_r = Q_w = 0$, and $\Delta = S_r L_w - S_w L_r$. From the result that $x_i = t_i = H_i - r$, it follows that $P_r = -S$ and $P_w = -(1 + n)L$. Therefore, the first-order conditions (31) become

(51.1) $\lambda \left[S \dfrac{L_w}{\Delta} - (1 + r)L \dfrac{L_r}{\Delta} \right]$

$\qquad\qquad + \mu \left[t_i - S \dfrac{L_w}{\Delta} + (1 + n)L \dfrac{L_r}{\Delta} \right] = 0$ $(i = 1,2)$

(51.2) $\lambda \left[-S \dfrac{S_w}{\Delta} + (1 + r)L \dfrac{S_r}{\Delta} \right]$

$\qquad\qquad + \mu \left[t_w(1 + n) + S \dfrac{S_w}{\Delta} - (1 + n)L \dfrac{S_r}{\Delta} \right] = 0$

(51.3) $\lambda \left[S \dfrac{L_w}{\Delta} - (1+r)L \dfrac{L_r}{\Delta} \right]$

$$+ \mu \left[(n-r) - S \dfrac{L_w}{\Delta} + (1+n)L \dfrac{L_r}{\Delta} \right] = 0.$$

As noted in the previous section, $t_1 = t_2$, and if bonds are available as an instrument, (51.3) applies, and this uniform tax on capital equals $n - r$.

Regardless of whether debt is present, (51.1) and (51.2) are valid, and may be combined with the revenue constraint to obtain expressions for the optimal taxes:[14]

(52.1) $t_r = \dfrac{1}{M} \left\{ R \left[\dfrac{(1+n)L_w}{(1+r)L} - \dfrac{(1+n)L_r}{S} \right] + (1+n)L \left(\dfrac{r-n}{1+r} \right) \right\}$

(52.2) $t_w = \dfrac{1}{M} \left\{ R \left[\dfrac{S_r}{S} - \dfrac{S_w}{(1+r)L} \right] - S \left(\dfrac{r-n}{1+r} \right) \right\},$

where $t_r = t_1 = t_2$ and

(53) $M = (1+n)L \left[\dfrac{S_r}{S} - \dfrac{S_w}{(1+r)L} \right] + S \left[\dfrac{(1+n)L_w}{(1+r)L} - \dfrac{(1+n)L_r}{S} \right].$

The optimal taxes depicted by (52) depend not only on the various factor supply derivatives, but also on the difference between the personal discount rate r and the social discount rate n.

If we ignore the divergence between r and n, then a familiar type of result follows. Let θ_r and θ_w be the ad valorem taxes corresponding to t_r and t_w, η_{ij} the factor supply elasticities, and α_s and α_L, the total returns to saving and labor. From (52) we obtain

(54) $$\dfrac{\theta_r}{\theta_w} = \dfrac{\alpha_L(\eta_{Lw}/\alpha_L - \eta_{Lr}/\alpha_s)}{\alpha_s(\eta_{sr}/\alpha_s - \eta_{sw}/\alpha_L)},$$

which if we ignore the cross-price effects, η_{Lr} and η_{sw}, yields the well-known "inverse-elasticity rule":[15]

(55) $$\dfrac{\theta_r}{\theta_w} = \dfrac{\eta_{Lw}}{\eta_{sr}},$$

which indicates that the optimal taxes should be inversely propor-

---

14. It may be verified using the Slutsky equation and equations (13) that equations (52) are equally valid when the uncompensated factor supply derivatives are replaced by their compensated counterparts.

15. See Bradford and Rosen [1976], for example, for the derivation of similar results.

tional to the elasticity of factor supply, and that if either factor is supplied inelastically, it should bear the entire tax.

Such optimal tax rules may alternatively be derived in a static context from the desire to minimize the excess burden that taxes induce by driving wedges between gross and net prices that, in the present case, are the wage rate and the interest rate. In our model, however, there is a third potential distortion—the use in individual savings decisions of a discount rate r, which differs from the social discount rate n. It is clear from (52) that this distortion influences t_r and t_w. Even with the debt instrument available, r will not equal n unless $t_r = 0$, which, in turn, occurs only if labor is supplied inelastically, taking account of cross-price effects.

These results may also be interpreted in terms of the demand for C_1, C_2, and $\tilde{L}$, rather than the supply of S and L. If we rearrange the budget constraint (11) as

$$(56) \qquad \frac{1}{w} C_1 + \frac{1}{w(1+r)} C_2 + (\tilde{L} - \overline{L}) = 0,$$

then it becomes clear that utility-maximizing consumers behave as if C_1 had a price $p_1 = w^{-1}$ and C_2 had a price $p_2 = [w(1+r)]^{-1}$, with leisure as numeraire.

Using the definitions of p_1 and p_2, the facts that $S = C_2/(1+r)$ and $L = \overline{L} - \tilde{L}$, the Slutsky equation and the symmetry property of compensated price derivatives, we may rewrite (52.1) as

$$(57) \qquad t_r = \frac{1}{M} \left[\frac{R(1+n)C_1}{(1+r)w^2 L} (\epsilon_{1\tilde{L}} - \epsilon_{2\tilde{L}}) + (1+n)L \left(\frac{r-n}{1+r} \right) \right],$$

where $\epsilon_{1\tilde{L}}$ and $\epsilon_{2\tilde{L}}$ are the compensated elasticities of first-period and second-period consumption with respect to the price of leisure. Again, this result differs from previous ones because of the difference between r and n. If we assume that $r = n$, we get the outcome referred to in the introduction, that t_r should diverge from zero only if either first-period or second-period consumption is a relative complement to leisure. If bonds are used optimally, then since $t_r = n - r$, we may be assured that $r = n$ if $\epsilon_{1\tilde{L}} = \epsilon_{2\tilde{L}}$.

It may be unrealistic to assume that government may be able to set debt at the optimal level specified by (51.3), especially if this level is negative. Thus, divergence from the "Golden Rule," which occurs if the effective discount rate, $r + t_r$, and hence the marginal product of capital, does not equal n, may have an important effect on optimal taxes. To illustrate this, we consider the case in which utility is

Cobb-Douglas, so that $S_r = L_w = L_r = 0$. With these simplifications, condition (52.1) becomes

$$(58) \qquad t_r = \frac{H_K - n}{1 - \sigma},$$

where $\sigma = S_w/L$ is the marginal propensity to save and $H_K = H_1 = H_2$ is the marginal product of capital. Unless the economy is following a "Golden Rule" path, it will be optimal to have a nonzero tax on capital, even though utility is separable, with this tax being positive when there is "too little" savings and $H_K > n$.[16]

VII. OPTIMAL CAPITAL TAXATION

In many situations it may be more appropriate to consider how best to tax capital, if other instruments are not available. In this section we consider again the special case in which neither type of capital depreciates, and ignore the possibility of government debt. We assume that the tax on labor income is exogenously set at a value $\bar{t}_w$.

Following the same argument as before, we differentiate the appropriate Lagrangean with respect to r and w instead of the taxes t_1 and t_2 themselves. Using equation (25) and the fact that $x_i = t_i = H_i - r$, we may express the first-order conditions as

$$(59.1) \qquad \lambda(1 + r)L$$

$$= \mu \left[(1 + n)L - t_1 \frac{dK_1}{dw} - t_2 \frac{dK_2}{dw} - \bar{t}_w(1 + n)L_w \right]$$

$$(59.2) \qquad \lambda S = \mu \left[S - t_1 \frac{dK_1}{dr} - t_2 \frac{dK_2}{dr} - \bar{t}_w(1 + n)L_r \right].$$

We must now solve for the derivatives of K_1 and K_2 with respect to r and w. We know by (25) that $H_3 = w + \bar{t}_w$. Since $\bar{t}_w$ is fixed, it follows that

$$(60) \qquad \frac{dH_3}{dr} = 0; \quad \frac{dH_3}{dw} = 1.$$

By using (14) and (28), and noting that $B = 0$ and $q_1 = q_2 = 1$, we obtain

$$(61) \qquad \frac{dK_1}{dr} + \frac{dK_2}{dr} = S_r; \quad \frac{dK_1}{dw} + \frac{dK_2}{dw} = S_w \qquad (i = 1,2).$$

16. Note that, as long as $0 < \sigma < 1$, $(H_k - n)$ and $(r - n)$ will have opposite signs. Thus, $r < n$ whenever $H_k > n$.

Totally differentiating H_3 with respect to r and w, we may then solve for the derivatives of K_1 and K_2 with respect to r and w by making use of (60) and (61). Doing so, we obtain

(62)

$$\frac{dK_1}{dr} = \frac{1}{D} [H_{32}S_r + H_{33}(1 + n)L_r];$$

$$\frac{dK_2}{dr} = -\frac{1}{D} [H_{31}S_r + H_{33}(1 + n)L_r];$$

$$\frac{dK_1}{dw} = \frac{1}{D} [H_{32}S_w + H_{33}(1 + n)L_w - 1];$$

$$\frac{dK_2}{dw} = -\frac{1}{D} [H_{31}S_w + H_{33}(1 + n)L_w - 1],$$

where $D = H_{32} - H_{31}$. Substituting (62) into conditions (59), we may simplify to obtain the optimal tax schedule. Combining equations (59.1) and (59.2), we get

(63) $$\frac{t_1}{D} \left[\frac{1}{S} (H_{32}S_r + H_{33}(1 + n)L_r) - \frac{1}{(1 + r)L} \right.$$

$$\times (H_{32}S_w + H_{33}(1 + n)L_w - 1) \Big]$$

$$- \frac{t_2}{D} \left[\frac{1}{S} (H_{31}S_r + H_{33}(1 + n)L_r) \right.$$

$$- \frac{1}{(1 + r)L} (H_{31}S_w + H_{33}(1 + n)L_w - 1) \Big]$$

$$= \frac{r - n}{1 + r} + \bar{t}_w \left[\frac{(1 + n)L_w}{(1 + r)L} - \frac{(1 + n)L_r}{S} \right].$$

Using the revenue constraint, (27) and (63), we may solve for t_1 and t_2. Since we are interested in the differential tax, we then subtract t_1 from t_2, getting Δt:

(64) $$\Delta t = D \left(\frac{M}{N} \right) \left\{ \frac{1}{M} \left[R \left(\frac{S_r}{S} - \frac{S_w}{(1 + r)L} \right) - S \left(\frac{r - n}{1 + r} \right) \right] - \bar{t}_w \right\},$$

where M is as defined in (53) and

$$
(65) \quad N = K_1 \left[\frac{1}{S} (H_{31}S_r + H_{33}(1+n)L_r) - \frac{1}{(1+r)L} \right.
$$

$$
\times (H_{31}S_w + H_{33}(1+n)L_w - 1) \Bigg]
$$

$$
+ K_2 \left[\frac{1}{S} (H_{32}S_r + H_{33}(1+n)L_r) \right.
$$

$$
- \frac{1}{(1+r)L} (H_{32}S_w + H_{33}(1+n)L_w - 1) \Bigg].
$$

We note that if $\bar{t}_w$ happens to equal the optimal labor income tax defined by (52.2), then $\Delta t = 0$. Generally, however, the term in brackets in (64) will not equal zero, being positive if $\bar{t}_w$ is "too low" and negative if it is "too high."

Given a non-optimal tax on labor income (and assuming that $M/N \neq 0$), the differential tax on capital will be nonzero as long as $D \neq 0$. This condition has a straightforward interpretation. The change in the marginal product of labor with respect to a change in capital of type i, which equals H_{3i}, is a measure of the complementarity in production of these factors. Thus, D will be positive if K_2 is "more" complementary to labor than K_1, and zero only if neither is a relative complement. D represents the change in the marginal product of labor arising from a shift of a unit of capital from use as K_1 to use as K_2. Since the tax on wages is fixed, the differential tax may be used as an alternative way of affecting w, but only if $D \neq 0$. In particular, if production may be represented by a function separable into capital and labor, condition (64) will be satisfied when $\Delta t = 0$. Suppose that

$$
(66) \qquad H(K_1, K_2, L) = G[\phi(K_1, K_2), L];
$$

then

$$
(67) \qquad \frac{H_1}{H_2} = \frac{G_\phi \phi_1}{G_\phi \phi_2} = \frac{\phi_1}{\phi_2} = \frac{G_{\phi L} \phi_1}{G_{\phi L} \phi_2} = \frac{H_{31}}{H_{32}} .
$$

If $t_1 = t_2$ ($\Delta t = 0$), it follows that $H_1 = H_2$ and, from (67), that $D = H_{32} - H_{31} = 0$, so that (64) is satisfied. This result bears an interesting similarity to that already mentioned above, dealing with the equality of excise taxes under conditions of separability of utility into taxed and untaxed commodities.

We now consider the sign of Δt. We may set $D > 0$ without any loss of generality, and examine the case where H_{31} and H_{32} are positive

and the tax on labor is too low. (The analysis is easily translated for other assumptions.) It then follows from (64) that it is optimal to set $\Delta t > 0$, that is, to tax more heavily capital more complementary to labor, if $M/N > 0$. In order to interpret this condition, we introduce the concept of an "allocation-neutral" tax change.

DEFINITION. Consider a change in the taxes, t_w, t_1, and t_2, which keeps utility constant. We call this shift "allocation-neutral" if the allocation of capital, measured by the value K_1/K_2, is unaffected.

This construct allows us to analyze the effect of a shift in the tax-assessed burden from labor to capital or vice versa.

By the competitive assumptions, we know that for any change in w, t_w must change according to

(68) $$\frac{dt_w}{dw} = \frac{dH_3}{dw} - 1.$$

Expanding dH_3/dw, we may rewrite (68) as

(69) $$\frac{dt_w}{dw} = H_{31}\frac{dK_1}{dw} + H_{32}\frac{dK_2}{dw} + H_{33}(1 + n)\frac{dL}{dw} - 1.$$

If the change in w is due to an allocation-neutral tax change, then K_1/K_2 is constant, so that (69) simplifies to

(70) $$\frac{dt_w^*}{dw} = \left(H_{31}\frac{K_1}{K} + H_{32}\frac{K_2}{K}\right)\frac{dK^*}{dw} + H_{33}(1 + n)\frac{dL^*}{dw} - 1,$$

where $K = K_1 + K_2 = S$ and the asterisk signifies that the change is allocation-neutral. The changes in K and L in (70) must obey

(71) $$\frac{dK^*}{dw} = S_w + S_r\frac{dr^*}{dw}; \qquad \frac{dL^*}{dw} = L_w + L_r\frac{dr^*}{dw}.$$

Since utility is held constant and since $S = K$, (13) implies that

(72) $$\frac{dr^*}{dw} = -\frac{(1 + r)L}{K}.$$

Substituting (72) into (71), combining this with (70), and comparing with (65) yields

(73) $$N = -\frac{K}{(1 + r)L}\frac{dt_w^*}{dw}.$$

Thus, N will be positive as long as an increase in t_w has the effect of depressing wages.

We may also rewrite M, using (71) and (72), as

(74) $$M = \frac{K}{(1 + r)L}\left[(1 + n)\frac{dL^*}{dw} - \frac{(1 + n)L}{K}\frac{dK^*}{dw}\right].$$

Combining (73) and (74) and noting that $(dw/dt_w)^* = 1/(dt_w/dw)^*$, we obtain

$$(75) \qquad \frac{M}{N} = (1 + n)L \frac{d \log (K/L)^*}{dt_w},$$

so that a shift in the assessed burden from capital to labor increases the capital-labor ratio if M/N is positive.

We may now intuitively explain the effect of M/N on the sign of the distortionary tax in (64). If the tax on labor is "too low," then K/L will be "too low" if $M/N > 0$. By taxing the capital complementary to labor, the differential tax Δt lowers the marginal product of labor, making labor less desirable in production relative to capital. If M/N is negative, this tax acts in the opposite direction. In either case the effect is to discourage the use of the factor that is being used "too much."

VIII. BEQUESTS AND THE DISCOUNT RATE

In this paper we have analyzed the nature of a steady state that would be relevant if society applied a discount rate n, equal to the population growth rate, to the aggregate utility of future generations. At the same time we have assumed that individuals leave no bequests. This issue merits further discussion, although a comprehensive treatment will not be attempted here.

Suppose that $r > n$ in equilibrium; then social welfare could be increased if every member of a given generation j saved an additional dollar out of first-period earnings, and the resulting $(1 + r)N_j$ dollars accruing in the next period were distributed equally to the $(1 + n)N_j$ members of generation $j + 1$. Since all individuals have the same marginal utility of first-period income in the steady state, the drop in per capita utility in generation j would be smaller than the gain in that of generation $j + 1$, and social welfare (see (5)) would increase. And yet, we have assumed that such transfers do not occur, even when $r > n$. There are various possible explanations that may be suggested. One is that the social welfare function described in (5) does not represent a simple aggregation of consumer preferences, but rather some ethical judgment of society. This notion is implicit in the argument made by Ramsey [1928] against the use of a pure rate of discount in the evaluation of consumption by future generations. The point is that while no member of the current generation need care about the welfare of anyone yet unborn, it would violate moral principles for the current generation to use up all of the world's resources and leave nothing for the future. A second argument, associated with Pigou [1920], is that

individuals may be myopic, so that government must act in the best interests of the population.

Marglin [1963] rejects explanations of the sort just discussed, suggesting that the provision for future generations through bequests may involve externalities that result in market failure. If every member of the current generation cares not only about his own children, but also about the children of others, and others care about his children or, more generally, if individuals care not only about their own descendants but also about the future welfare of society as a whole, then bequests will generate externalities, and individuals will not take account of all of the social benefit that would result from a potential bequest. Thus, even if r exceeds a unanimously agreed-upon social discount rate, a bequest's perceived net benefit from the individual point of view may be negative, in which case no bequests would occur. Thus, we may interpret the divergence of r and n in our economy as coming from such an externality, and the optimal taxes that are called for as acting, in part, to correct this externality.

If no such externality is present, and individuals each have a welfare function like (5) relating their own utility to that of their descendants, it is clear that, in the steady state, $r = n$ as long as bequests are positive. The results of Sections VI and VII may be extended to consider this possibility. It turns out to be a straightforward process to demonstrate that the optimal taxes which result are those called for by the existing formulas when the savings elasticity with respect to the interest rate is infinite, $S_r = \infty$. Thus, for the case in which t_1, t_2, and t_w may all be adjusted, (52.1) yields

$$(76) \qquad\qquad\qquad t_r = 0$$

so that only labor should be taxed. For the case in which only t_1 and t_2 may be adjusted, (63) yields

$$(77) \qquad\qquad\qquad \frac{t_1}{t_2} = \frac{H_{31}}{H_{32}}.$$

Assuming that H_{31} and H_{32} are both positive, we see that it will be optimal to tax more heavily labor's relative complement if the tax on labor is low and capital must face a positive tax, and to tax more heavily labor's relative substitute if the tax on labor is too high and capital income of each kind is subsidized.

IX. CONCLUSION

In this paper we have explored the issue of optimal capital taxation, taking into consideration the characteristics of capital goods

themselves and how they enter into the production process, under various assumptions concerning the availability of instruments to the government. We have found that it will generally be optimal to tax capital differentially, even when the tax on labor income may be adjusted freely, unless capital services follow a pattern of exponential decay or the economy is on a "Golden Rule" path. If government bonds are available, they may be used to obtain the latter of these conditions.

When capital of each type is assumed to be homogeneous and nondepreciating, the taxes on capital, which are uniform, and that on labor differ from those suggested by static optimal tax theory due to a potential divergence between the private and social discount rates. If the kind of externality that might give rise to such a divergence is ruled out, then the optimal tax on capital income is zero.

If only taxes on capital are available, it will generally be optimal to set them at different rates, even when capital is nondepreciating, unless production may be expressed as a function separable into capital and labor.

REFERENCES

Arrow, K. J., and M. Kurz, *Public Investment, the Rate of Return and Optimal Fiscal Policy* (Baltimore: Johns Hopkins Press, 1970).

Atkinson, A. B., and J. E. Stiglitz, "The Design of Tax Structure: Direct versus Indirect Taxation," *Journal of Public Economics*, V (Aug. 1976), 55–75.

Auerbach, A. J., "Neutrality and the Corporate Tax," HIER Discussion Paper #657, October, 1978.

——, "Inflation and the Choice of Asset Life," *Journal of Political Economy*, LXXXIX (June 1979), 621–38.

Bradford, D. F., and H. S. Rosen, "The Optimal Taxation of Commodities and Income," *American Economic Review LXVI* (May 1976), 94–109.

Diamond, P. A., "Debt in a Neoclassical Growth Model," *American Economic Review* LV, (Dec. 1965), 1126–50.

——, "Taxation and Public Production in a Growth Setting," in J. A. Mirrlees and N. H. Stern, eds., *Models of Economic Growth* (London: Macmillan, 1973).

——, and J. A. Mirrlees, "Optimal Taxation and Public Production," *American Economic Review*, LXI (March and June 1971), 8–27 and 261–78.

Feldstein, M. S., "The Welfare Cost of Capital Income Taxation," *Journal of Political Economy*, LXXXVIII (April 1978), S29–S51.

Hahn, F. H., "Equilibrium Dynamics with Heterogeneous Capital Goods," this *Journal*, LXXX (Nov. 1966), 633–46.

Harberger, A. C., "Taxation, Resource Allocation and Welfare," in J. Due, ed., *The Role of Direct and Indirect Taxes in the Federal Revenue System* (Princeton: NBER, 1964).

——, "Efficiency Effects of Taxes on Income from Capital," in M. Krzyzaniak, ed., *Effects of the Corporation Income Tax* (Detroit: Wayne State University Press, 1966).

Intriligator, M. D., *Mathematical Optimization and Economic Theory* (Englewood Cliffs, N.J.: Prentice-Hall, 1971).

Marglin, S. A., "The Social Rate of Discount and the Optimal Rate of Investment," this *Journal*, LXXVII (Feb. 1963), 95–111.

Pestieau, P., "Optimal Taxation and Discount Rate for Public Investment," *Journal of Public Economics*, II (Aug. 1974), 217–35.

Phelps, E. S., "The Golden Rule of Accumulation: A Fable for Growthmen," *American Economic Review*, LI (Sept. 1961), 638–43.

Pigou, A. C., *The Economics of Welfare* (London: Macmillan, 1920).

Ramsey, F. P., "A Mathematical Theory of Saving," *Economic Journal*, XXXVIII (Dec. 1928), 543–59.

Robinson, J., "A Neo-Classical Theorem," *Review of Economic Studies*, XXIX (June 1962), 219–26.

Samuelson, P. A., "Tax Deductibility of Economic Depreciation to Insure Invariant Valuations," *Journal of Political Economy*, LXXII (Dec. 1964), 604–06.

Sandmo, A., "A Note on the Structure of Optimal Taxation," *American Economic Review*, LXIV (Sept. 1974), 701–06.

Shell, K., and J. E. Stiglitz, "The Allocation of Investment in a Dynamic Economy," this *Journal*, LXXXI (Nov. 1967), 592–609.

2
Tax Neutrality and the Social Discount Rate

1. Introduction

There are few problems in tax analysis which have generated as much study and discussion among economists as the question of how to formulate 'neutral' tax incentives for investment. This concentration of research effort may be traced to the importance and relevance to policy design of the issues under investigation. In this light, it is especially distressing to the economist and government planner alike that no consensus has been reached concerning the proper approach to take when adjusting taxes. On the contrary, authors continue to analyze the problem of investment incentives using distinct criteria, each calling markedly different tax schemes neutral. In each case, satisfaction of the neutrality criterion is argued to lead to an efficient allocation of capital, but this cannot be simultaneously true for different criteria.

A problem in assessing the validity of these arguments is that an underlying model of optimizing behavior is rarely developed, so that claims of efficiency are hard to contradict. In principle, such difficulties could be avoided by simply considering the design of investment incentives in a full

This paper is a substantially revised version of one originally issued as a Harvard and NBER Working Paper. I have benefited from discussions with several colleagues and the opportunity to present this paper in seminars at Harvard, NBER, and the SSRC Public Sector Economics .Study Group.

model of optimal taxation. However, the information requirements of such a procedure make it impractical, and we must ask whether it is possible to develop a simpler framework still grounded in welfare theory to be used in evaluating a tax system. This paper attempts to develop such a framework.

To define the problem, we first present and compare the two fundamental notions of neutrality found in the literature, which we refer to as Present Value (PV) Rules and Internal Rate of Return (IRR) Rules.[1] Section 3 reviews the meaning of production efficiency in an intertemporal context, and shows that only the IRR approach can be consistent with the efficient allocation of capital.

The potential attainment of production efficiency does not constitute a complete argument for using the IRR approach to neutrality. In section 4, we evaluate this issue more fully by developing the idea of a 'value equivalent' investment program, and relate the neutrality question to the literature on optimal taxation and the choice of discount rate for public projects. Our conclusion is that the usefulness of the IRR concept of neutrality depends on what instruments the government is assumed to have at its disposal, but that it may constitute a sensible rule of thumb under conditions which typically prevail.

2. Tax neutrality

The problem normally posed is that the government planner confronts an existing and, perhaps, ill-conceived tax system and must, within some bounds involving short-run and possibly long-run revenue loss limits, decide how to change the tax treatment of a specified group of assets to accomplish the objective of greater capital investment. The reason for the proposed stimulus is a perceived need for more capital (because the existing tax law has heretofore unduly discouraged accumulation).[2] The analysis compares the effect of proposed tax changes on assets of different durability to ascertain whether the resulting tax system will 'favor' long-lived or short-lived assets, the reference point being either the initial tax system or, more commonly, the hypothetical no-tax case. The ultimate tax scheme is neutral if it favors neither more durable nor less durable assets. It is the way in

---

[1] The distinction here will turn out to be between two methods of discounting, and is unrelated to the long-standing dispute over whether to choose projects according to present values or internal rates of return. The terminology used here follows that of the relevant literature.

[2] At least in the past, a second reason for initiating investment incentives has been to stimulate aggregate demand during a recession. See Gordon and Jorgenson (1976). However, as argued by Lucas (1976), if such is the avowed purpose of the incentives, the analysis must take into account the likelihood that investors will anticipate tax changes. Furthermore, the impact of such expectations differs across investments of different durability. See Auerbach (1978).

which the tax system's effects are measured that the two approaches mentioned above differ.

To facilitate the explanation of these measures, we use the familiar 'user cost of capital' [Jorgenson (1963)] which describes the implicit rental price of capital which depreciates exponentially. It is this shadow price to which firms equate the marginal product of capital of the type in question. While we will eventually relax the restrictive assumption of geometric decay, it is acceptable for the present purpose of illustration. Without loss of generality, we ignore presonal taxes and inflation, and assume only equity finance (or, equivalently, no deductibility of interest).[3] We also assume perfect certainty to prevail.

Letting δ be the decay rate of capital (at time t after purchase, a fraction $e^{-\delta t}$ of the initial asset remains), $p(\delta)$ the price of such capital in units of output, τ the corporate tax rate, $k(\delta)$ the tax credit on gross investment, r the required return on equity (taken to be the interest rate), and

$$z(\delta) = \int_0^\infty e^{-rt} D(\delta,t)\, dt \tag{1}$$

the present value of depreciation allowances $\{D(\delta,t)\}$ arising over time from an initial one dollar purchase of an asset with decay rate δ, the user cost of capital is

$$c(\delta) = p(\delta)(r+\delta)(1-k(\delta)-\tau z(\delta))/(1-\tau). \tag{2}$$

At the margin, the gross return to a unit of capital of type δ must equal $c(\delta)$, and the corresponding net return, after taxes, equals $r \cdot p(\delta)$ plus depreciation.

2.1. Present value rules

This approach has actually been formulated in two different ways in the literature. Some authors [Sunley (1973), Sandmo (1974), Kopcke (1981)] have formulated the criterion in terms of the tax system's impact on user cost, others [Black (1959), Boadway (1978)] have made reference to the present value of gross returns associated with each asset.

The first of these approaches defines as neutral a tax system which exerts the same proportional influence on user costs associated with different assets, implying that the ratio of user cost with taxes to user cost without taxes,

$$\bar{c}(\delta) = \frac{p(\delta)(r+\delta)(1-k(\delta)-\tau z(\delta))/(1-\tau)}{p(\delta)(r+\delta)} = \frac{1-k(\delta)-\tau z(\delta)}{1-\tau}, \tag{3}$$

---

[3] All that will really be necessary for these simplifications not to matter is that there be no systematic relationship between the type of asset and the method with which it is financed or the personal tax rates of its owners. For a more general derivation of user cost see Auerbach (1981b).

is constant.[4,5] It is not entirely clear what motivates this conception of tax neutrality, though under certain restrictions on the production technology it may be shown that the relative intensity of use of two kinds of capital depends only on the ratio of their associated user costs.[6] However, even if this is so, there is no reason why one should care to preserve any particular pattern of relative use. For example, in an economy without taxes or externalities satisfying the requirements for Pareto-optimality, a change in tastes or technology might lead to a change in the interest rate. This would change $c(\delta)$ proportionately more for longer-lived assets, but the new outcome would still be Pareto-optimal.

The alternative and, as it turns out, equivalent formulation suggests that a tax system is neutral if, at the margin, all investments of equal initial cost have the same present value when their gross returns are discounted at r. Since the gross return to a marginal investment at any point in time equals the cost of capital multiplied by the amount of captial remaining, the present value of gross returns to an initial one dollar invested in capital of type δ is

$$\mathrm{pv}(\delta) = \int_0^\infty e^{-rt} c(\delta) \left(\frac{e^{-\delta t}}{p(\delta)}\right) \mathrm{d}t = \frac{1 - k(\delta) - \tau z(\delta)}{1 - \tau} = \bar{c}(\delta). \tag{4}$$

Since the present value of net-of-tax returns must, by definition and regardless of tax regime, equal one dollar for each marginal project, the requirement that $\mathrm{pv}(\delta)$ be constant over δ is equivalent to the condition that the present value of taxes collected from each dollar invested (the difference between the present value of gross flows and the present value of net flows) be independent of the type of project chosen.

A representative justification for this approach has been offered by Boadway (1978); 'Capital at any instant will be allocated efficiently if the value of its marginal product is the same in all uses where the value of its marginal product is the present value of the contribution of an increment of capital investment now to output in the future.' At first, this argument may seem convincing — equating marginal products of a factor in all uses is a

---

[4] An alternative way of stating the criterion would be that, starting from a no-tax equilibrium, changes in the tax law exert an equiproportional influence on the different user costs. However, this would require the tax changes to depend on general equilibrium changes in the interest rate. Phrasing the criterion as we have is consistent with the normal approach which does not consider changes in r.

[5] Feldstein (1981) has phrased this criterion in terms of the proportional effect of the tax system of $[1 - k(\delta) - \tau z(\delta)]$, which he refers to as the 'net cost of investment'.

[6] If the technology is characterized by a production function, $F(\cdot)$ of the two capital goods, K_1 and K_2, and all other factors, M, satisfying

$$F(K_1, K_2; M) = G(\phi(K_1, K_2); M),$$

where ϕ is homogeneous in its arguments, than K_2/K_1 may be expressed as a monotonically increasing function of c_1/c_2 alone. Indeed, if F is not restricted in this way, an increase in c_1 could occasion a relative increase in K_1.

basic requirement for efficiency, after all — but one must examine carefully the assumption upon which it is based: that in comparing the returns from different projects it is admissible to aggregate flows from a given project by discounting them with the consumption rate of discount, r, making no further adjustments to the flows according to the source of investment funds or the eventual destination and use of investment proceeds.[7] The justification for this procedure has been explored in the social discount rate literature [Arrow (1966), Kay (1972)], with the finding that it is valid only if one assumes that the rate of savings out of net project flows is independent of when or in what form these flows occur. There may be cases where this extreme type of constrained behavior is defensible as an assumption. However, it seems entirely inappropriate for the analysis of the choice of private investment projects, since it implies that the intertemporal consumption decisions of a firm's owners depend on the durability of its capital stock. If the firm invests in a very short-lived asset, which yields flows over a brief period of time, the stockholders are presumed to consume the same fraction of this return as they would of a much smaller flow coming over a longer period from a more durable asset of equal value. It seems more reasonable to assume that the rate of saving would be inversely related to the durability of the asset, in which case the simple present value rule stated above is inapplicable.

2.2. Internal rate of return rules

Perhaps the more common view of neutrality is based on internal rates of return on different assets. A tax system is viewed as neutral if the internal rates of return calculated from the gross returns of each marginal project are equal [Musgrave (1959), Chase (1962), Tideman (1975), Sunley (1976), Auerbach (1979a), Bradford (1980), Harberger (1980)]. Given the assumption of geometric decay, this gross internal rate of return for a project of type δ, $\rho(\delta)$, is defined by the equation

$$\int_0^\infty e^{-\rho(\delta)t} c(\delta) e^{-\delta t} \, dt = p(\delta), \tag{5}$$

which yields the solution for the internal rate of return to be kept constant over δ:

$$\rho(\delta) = \frac{c(\delta)}{p(\delta)} - \delta = \frac{(r+\delta)(1 - k(\delta) - \tau z(\delta))}{1 - \tau} - \delta. \tag{6}$$

[7] There are other problems with the present value approach, or at least its implementation, discussed in Auerbach (1981a).

As in the previous case, this approach may also be phrased in terms of tax liability. Since after-tax flows from a project must yield an internal rate of return equal to r, requiring $\rho(\delta)$ to be constant is equivalent to requiring a single effective tax rate on all assets, where such a rate is defined as the difference between gross and net rates of return divided by the gross rate, $(\rho(\delta) - r)/\rho(\delta)$.

The motivation behind this criterion is also the idea that capital should have the same marginal product in all uses to insure efficiency. However, the use of internal rates of return in the choice of investment projects has been subject to the following criticism: 'It is well known that only when the internal rate of return equals the discount rate will the present value of two projects with the same internal rate of return be the same . . . Therefore, this criterion of neutrality has no basis in welfare economics' [Boadway (1978)].

From (4) and (6), it follows that

$$pv(\delta) = (\rho(\delta) + \delta)/(r + \delta), \tag{7}$$

so that if the internal rate of return criterion is satisfied, the present value criterion must be violated unless $\rho(\delta) \equiv r$ or, trivially, δ is the same for all assets. However, this criticism of the IRR approach rests on the assumption that individual assets are the appropriate units of comparison, an assumption we have just challenged in relation to the PV approach. We return to this issue in section 3.

2.3. An example

From (7), we know that these two views of what constitutes a neutral tax incentive are not the same, but an example will help to demonstrate how different they are. For simplicity, we assume the initial tax system consists of a corporate tax with no investment tax credit, and that depreciation allowances correspond to economic depreciation.[8] It is relatively easy to show, in this case, that the value of a unit of capital of type δ initially purchased at time zero for one dollar equals $e^{-\delta t}$,[9] so that instantaneous depreciation at time t is $\delta e^{-\delta t}$, and the present value of depreciation allowances is

$$z(\delta) = \int_0^\infty e^{-rt} \delta e^{-\delta t} \, dt = \frac{\delta}{r + \delta}. \tag{8}$$

---

[8] Economic depreciation is defined as the decline in value of an asset, and depends not only on the rate of physical decay but on the tax system itself.

[9] Note that this result depends on the assumption that depreciation allowances in fact do follow economic depreciation. If, for example, depreciation allowances were accelerated, capital value at time t would be less than $e^{-\delta t}$.

The values for the user cost, $c(\delta)$, and the measures $pv(\delta)$ and $\rho(\delta)$ are:

$$c(\delta) = p(\delta)\left(\frac{r}{1-\tau} + \delta\right), \tag{9a}$$

$$pv(\delta) = \left(\frac{r}{1-\tau} + \delta\right) \Big/ (r+\delta), \tag{9b}$$

$$\rho(\delta) = \frac{r}{1-\tau}. \tag{9c}$$

In terms of taxes, the present value of taxes collected from a one dollar investment in an asset of type δ is $\tau/(1-\tau) \cdot r/(r+\delta)$, whereas the effective tax rate is simply τ. Thus, the system is neutral by the rate of return criterion, but favors short-lived assets according to the other view, since $d\, pv(\delta)/d\delta < 0$.

To fully appreciate the difficulty faced by the planner uncertain about which approach to take, suppose he is' now asked to introduce a 'neutral' investment tax credit to the system. Letting $k(0)$ be the credit applicable for assets which do not decay ($\delta = 0$), the shape of such a credit over δ would be

$$k(\delta) = k(0) - \tau\frac{\delta}{r+\delta} \tag{10a}$$

by the present value criterion, but

$$k(\delta) = k(0) \cdot \left(1 - \frac{\delta}{r+\delta}\right) \tag{10b}$$

by the rate of return criterion. Table 1 presents sample values for these two functions for $\tau = 0.5,\cdot k(0) = 0.10$ and $r = 0.05$. These results demonstrate that these two approaches to neutrality dictate vastly different tax policies.[10]

3. Production efficiency

A problem with most previous attempts[11] to relate concepts of neutrality and production efficiency has been the failure to understand the meaning of production efficiency in a multi-period context. In a one-period model with a single, homogeneous output good, production efficiency certainly calls for factors to be allocated in a way that equates marginal products for each

---

[10] A recent example in the U.S. is the evaluation of the Conable–Jones proposal, which would shorten tax lifetimes to five and ten years for equipment and plant, respectively. Feldstein (1981) finds such a proposal reasonable under the present value criterion (see footnote 5) while Auerbach and Jorgenson (1980) find it to be even less neutral than current practice, using the effective tax rate as their measure.

[11] Bradford (1980) is a notable exception.

Table 1

A neutral investment tax
credit: Two views ($\tau =$
$0.5, k(0) = 0.10, r = 0.05$).

δ	PV	IRR
0	0.10	0.10
0.05	−0.15	0.05
0.10	−0.23	0.03
0.20	−0.30	0.02
∞	−0.40	0.00

factor across different potential uses. Indeed, if all capital goods lasted for one period, both approaches to neutrality discussed above would yield this outcome. However, when consumption occurs over time, consumption goods produced in different periods, even if alike in all other respects, are different commodities, and production efficiency is violated only if it is possible to replace a given production plan with one which allows more consumption in some periods, with at least as much in all others. This may strike some readers as trivial and quite obvious, but it is overlooked whenever a comparison is made of 'the' rate of return on multi-period assets, be it through 'calculation of a present value or an internal rate of return.

A simple example should serve to illustrate this point. Suppose there are three dates, labelled 0. 1, and 2, at which consumption can occur and that there is an endowment of date 0 consumption goods and two technologies, labelled A and B, which can convert consumption at date 0 into consumption at dates 1 and 2. Suppose technology A can produce consumption at date 1 only, and technology B can produce consumption at date 2 only. If no additional technology exists, it can make no sense to say that production of more date 1 goods and less date 2 goods represents an increase or decrease in production efficiency, assuming each technology itself is operated efficiently; all feasible combinations of A and B are efficient. If a third technology, C, is present which converts date 1 goods into date 2 goods, production efficiency then requires that the marginal rate of transformation from date 0 goods to date 2 goods be the same for technology B and the combination of A and C, if both methods are in use.

To return to the matter at hand, a comparison of technologies A and B, either by calculation of present values or internal rates of return, has nothing to do with production efficiency. The appropriate comparison is between B and the *combination* of A and C, and here either method of evaluation would do, as the two marginal rates of transformation of date 0

goods to date 2 goods will be equal if and only if each measure is the same across techniques.

Nevertheless, the IRR approach of comparing the single technologies A and B will yield the correct result if a further assumption is made, namely that the internal rate of return is the same for A and C individually, and hence the combination of A and C. Given that discussions of neutrality normally make such a stationarity assumption, it is not misleading to associate the IRR approach with production efficiency. Moreover, this result generalizes to comparisons of investments with arbitrary service patterns, as long as stationarity is assumed. It must be emphasized that no comparable claim can be made for the PV approach.

An entirely different matter from the correct definition of production efficiency is whether such efficiency is desirable. Here, it is crucial what instruments the government is assumed to be able to use. As Diamond and Mirrlees (1971) have shown, efficiency is socially optimal when all flows between household and production sectors may be taxed. However, this is not the problem normally facing the planner of investment incentives. In the next section we introduce the concept of a 'value-equivalent' program which is useful in extending this section's simple example to account for general types of investment good and in exploring the desirability of production efficiency under various assumptions about the availability of instruments to the government.

4. A suggested framework

In this section we focus on the marginal choice of a firm among different types of asset, maintaining the simplifying assumptions of all equity finance and no personal taxes or inflation. We imagine output in each period as being homogeneous. It can be used for consumption or invested for future consumption in any of several available technologies. In asking whether different investments should face the same effective tax rate and hence yield the same internal rate of return, we are considering a question related to the one familiar from the literature on public expenditure discounting, whether public projects should be discounted at the rate of return on similar private projects. The answer in that context, although also subject to a great deal of confusion, depends largely on what instruments the government is assumed to control. Under the assumptions of Diamond and Mirrlees (1971), the discount rates should be the same. Under the alternative assumption that the discount rate used in the private sector may be not fully controlled and diverges from the rate of time preference (perhaps because of a tax on capital income), a weighted average of the two may be appropriate [Sandmo and Drèze (1971)], though even this approach becomes complicated when there are more than two periods and has been criticized as inadequate as a

general rule [Drèze (1974), Feldstein (1974)]. The range of cases we consider is intermediate between these two extremes. While we do not assume that all commodity and factor tax rates are being set optimally, we will assume government possesses the ability to directly influence the discount rate on all types of investment. In the public–private context, this would amount to government being able to influence directly the amount of private investment displaced by public investment by adjusting the tax on private investment. In the current context, it corresponds to the ability to adjust effective tax rates on all, rather than just some, investments.

The analysis begins with the introduction of a useful construct. Because our focus is on the ability of government to control allocation in a decentralized market system, we examine the effect of different tax policies in the context of a household which chooses its investment plan to support a certain pattern of consumption.

A value-equivalent investment program will be defined as one in which a dollar is initially invested in a particular type of capital, and the after-tax proceeds retained and reinvested in the same type of asset or distributed to stockholders in such a way as to keep the total value of the investment at each instant consistent with some predetermined schedule. It follows that the schedule of after-tax distributions from any value-equivalent program must be identical. Letting V_t be the value of any program at time t, equilibrium requires that the after tax distribution be

$$E_t = rV_t - \dot{V}_t, \tag{11}$$

where $\dot{V}_t$ is the instantaneous change in the program's value. Since V and $\dot{V}$ are assumed not to vary by type of asset, neither can E.

Thus, the value-equivalent program may be thought of as the pattern of investment in a particular kind of capital necessary to provide a certain pattern of consumption. We may envision an investor as choosing among such programs to finance future consumption.[12] At the margin, of course, the choice of program is a matter of indifference to the consumer. However, the government (and hence society as a whole) may not be indifferent among the streams of tax receipts each program generates, and may wish to alter the tax system to encourage certain types of investment.

Throughout our discussion, we shall concentrate on the particular value-equivalent schedule which keeps the value of invested capital constant at one dollar, though this is done for the sake of simplicity and is not restrictive. It is important to remember that the equivalence across different programs is in terms of market value, taking account of tax rules, and not necessarily any other measure, like gross output. The constant value as-

---

[12]The assumption that each possible value-equivalent program is composed of homogeneous assets is made merely for expositional purposes. The arguments which follow could be applied as well to heterogeneous programs.

sumption implies a distribution of r dollars to the stockholders at each point in time, regardless of which kind of capital is utilized.

Unlike most previous analyses, ours will apply to assets with all types of service pattern. However, for illustrative purposes and to permit comparison with previous work, we begin with the assumption that each asset declines in productivity at some geometric rate, and consider the special case examined in the example in section 2, where depreciation allowances follow economic depreciation and there is no investment tax credit. In this case, the cost of capital for an asset of type δ is described in (9a), and the rate of economic depreciation is just the decay rate, δ. Thus, keeping the value of the total investment constant at a dollar will require a constant reinvestment rate of δ. To verify that this is correct we note that the distribution equals the gross return, less taxes, plus tax deductions for depreciation, less reinvestment, or:

$$\frac{c(\delta)}{p(\delta)}(1-\tau)+\tau\delta-\delta = \left(\frac{r}{1-\tau}+\delta\right)(1-\tau)+\tau\delta-\delta = r, \tag{12}$$

as is required.

Next, consider the corresponding stream of tax receipts coming from this asset. The government gets a constant flow of

$$R(\delta) = \tau\left(\frac{c(\delta)}{p(\delta)}-\delta\right) = \left(\frac{\tau}{1-\tau}\right)r. \tag{13}$$

Since the flows are equal for different assets and constant over time, it is clear that production efficiency is satisfied. A fortiori, if the tax rate differed across assets, the government's receipts would be permanently higher for an asset with a higher tax rate. Since investors are indifferent, it would seem socially preferable as well as efficient in the production sense to remove such differences by equalizing tax rates. This would then presumably constitute the 'neutral' tax policy for the government to use. Though the above result is for the special case of geometric decay, it can be shown to hold for value-equivalent programs composed of any type of capital investment, geometric or not, as long as the same tax system as in the case just considered applies.

Let A_t be the gross return before reinvestment at time t for an arbitrary such program. Note that A_t is not the flow from the initial one dollar investment, but that amount plus the flows from all subsequent investments undertaken to keep the total value of capital in the program equal to one dollar.[13] Let D_t and D_t' be the corresponding values of economic deprecia-

---

[13] Except where physical and economic depreciation coincide (which occurs only if there is geometric decay) A_t will fluctuate over time even though net consumption from the program does not. For example, if the capital goods in question follow the 'one-hoss shay' service pattern of constant flows for a time followed by complete decay, A_t will initially rise over time as the ratio of depreciation to gross returns rises.

tion and depreciation permitted under law. If τ is the applicable tax rate, it must be true that

$$r = (1 - \tau)A_t + \tau D_t' - D_t. \tag{14a}$$

That is, the after tax distribution equals r. Tax receipts are

$$R_t = \tau(A_t - D_t'). \tag{14b}$$

If the depreciation deductions correspond to economic depreciation for each investment and, hence, for each program as well, eqs. (14a) and (14b) become

$$r = (1 - \tau)(A_t - D_t) \tag{15a}$$

and

$$R_t = \tau(A_t - D_t), \tag{15b}$$

so that $R_t = \tau/(1 - \tau)r$, a constant. As is evident from comparing the constants r and R_t, the statutory tax rate is the effective tax rate whenever economic depreciation is permitted. As in the special case of geometric decay, the government's revenue stream can be made permanently higher if effective tax rates are unequal across assets, and production efficiency again appears to be desirable.

Lest it appear that this desirability of equal effective tax rates holds only when such rates are also equal to the statutory tax rate, consider the case of immediate expensing, where investment is written off upon purchase and there are no further depreciation deductions. For a typical value-equivalent investment program, the private investor puts up one dollar. Because assets are immediately expensed, this permits a purchase of $1/(1 - \tau)$ dollars worth of capital, with the government contributing a fraction τ of this amount through the deduction. Thereafter, since in the program economic depreciation and expenditures on new capital are at all times the same, the private distribution and government tax revenue at time t are still described by (15a) and (15b), respectively. Thus, the government's revenue stream consists of an initial cost, $\tau/(1 - \tau)$ followed by a constant revenue flow of $\tau/(1 - \tau)r$, regardless of the type of asset. Once again, the government's revenue stream is maximized when τ is set equal on all assets. However, here, the effective tax rates, though equal, do not equal τ, but zero, since from an initial total investment of $1/(1 - \tau)$ each program yields a gross annual flow of

$$r\left(1 + \frac{\tau}{1 - \tau}\right) = r\left(\frac{1}{1 - \tau}\right).$$

A simple extension of the above results is that any effective tax rate between τ and zero can be obtained through a combination of economic depreciation and expensing, with statutory and effective tax rates equal

across asset types. To see this, note that permitting expensing of a fraction α of gross investment leads to a constant tax revenue stream of $\tau/(1-\tau)r$ after an initial cost of $\alpha\tau/(1-\alpha\tau)$ to the government. This is still independent of asset type, and the effective tax rate is easily calculated to be $\tau(1-\alpha)/(1-\alpha\tau)$.[14]

We have thus far shown that for an important class of tax regimes, and regardless of asset type, choosing to set effective tax rates equal results not only in production efficiency, but leads as well to the outcome that government revenues, period-by-period, are higher than under inefficient production plans. This feature is important because no assumption need be made about the availability to the government of debt to transfer resources from one period to the next to say that the efficient outcome dominates others.

Nevertheless, this partial equilibrium approach (common to the literature on neutrality) does obscure other reasons why production efficiency may still be suboptimal. We have implicitly ignored what happens to the rest of the economy when tax rates on capital are adjusted. In the language of the discounting literature, we have found that if one type of investment displaces another type dollar for dollar, then the second investment should face the same discount rate (the 'social opportunity cost') as the first.

Is this an appropriate assumption in the current context? Suppose, for example, that one type of capital good may be more complementary to labor in production than the other type. Then this reallocation of capital to increase production efficiency, and hence the stream of government receipts, will have, except in two cases, the additional effect of changing the wage rate and hence the level of saving and consumption in different periods. The two cases where this indirect effect can be ignored are when wage taxes can be simultaneously and optimally adjusted (this follows from the Diamond–Mirrlees result) or when labor is of equal complementarity to the two capital goods [Auerbach (1979b)]. Neither of these is likely to be true in any realistic situation, especially as we enrich the model to include several types of labor and consumption. In principle, then, the optimal tax schedule will diverge from production efficiency.

Practically viewed, though, it is extremely difficult even in a very simple model to calculate merely the *direction* this divergence in effective tax rates should take.[15] Under real world 'nth best' conditions, and given this section's findings, there seems to be a strong argument for maintaining equal effective tax rates. Short of solving the full optimal tax problem, there is certainly no other rule of thumb which presents itself as an alternative.

[14] See Auerbach (1979a) or Harberger (1980) for a further discussion of this approach to incentives.

[15] In Auerbach (1979b), an explicit solution for the optimal tax rates on two capital goods is obtained, but it is quite complicated and the optimal divergence in tax rates depends in a very complicated way on the structure of preferences and technology.

However, the typical real-world tax code is more formidable than those examined in this section; it is rife with investment tax credits, accelerated depreciation allowances and the use of nominal rather than real bases to calculate tax liabilities in the presence of inflation. In general, D_t and D'_t need bear little systematic relationship over time or across assets and government may have the power to change effective tax rates on assets only by limited means, such as a change in asset lives or the investment tax credit. Thus, government receipts from different value-equivalent programs may have markedly different patterns, and this would appear to weaken the arguments in favor of production efficiency, which would still require setting equal all effective tax rates. Here, the role of debt is important.

5. Neutrality and the government discount rate

To restate this problem more formally, suppose two value-equivalent investment programs yield, under a particular tax system, streams of returns $\{R_t\}$ and $\{R_t^*\}$ to the government in the form of tax revenue. Ruling out the cases where one stream is uniformly bigger than the other, can we still determine which stream the government will prefer? If so, is there any simple criterion concerning the tax system which will lead to an outcome in which neither stream is preferred to the other, so that no reallocation of investment would be desirable? We shall argue in this section that the answer to each of these questions is yes, and that the criterion is the same as that which has proved appropriate in the case of economic depreciation allowances considered above.

We assume the government can issue debt, which as an asset is a perfect substitute for real capital and thus yields a net rate of return equal to r. This assumption is crucial, for were it not made, the timing of government expenditures would depend on the pattern of tax receipts.[16] Hence, a comparison of streams of tax receipts would have to account for the preferences of society concerning public sector expenditures. With the existence of government debt, we may simply ask whether, given a stream of government expenditures, $\{X_t\}$, a particular stream of tax receipts, $\{R_t\}$, is sufficient to fund it in the sense that any debt arising from the matching of tax receipts to public expenditures is eventually paid off.

---

[16] A second role for debt in achieving a social optimum would arise if there were intergenerational externalities and individual and social discount rates differed even in the absence of taxes. In overlapping-generations models, where individuals have finite horizons and leave no bequests, debt could be used to increase (or decrease) the economy's capital intensity as a remedy for this externality. This issue has been discussed in the discounting literature by Marglin (1963) and, more recently, in relation to the optimal tax problem by Auerbach (1979b) and Atkinson and Sandmo (1980). No such externality is assumed to exist in the current paper, although our analysis could be applied to that case by assuming first that to the extent that this externality might initially exist debt policy would be used to correct it.

We assume that the private capital displaced by the sale of government debt is always a representative mixture of the investments in society, and take this 'composite capital' to be the same over time and have a gross internal rate of return equal to $r/(1-u)$. Except for ownership, the outcome of this process will be identical to one in which, rather than selling or repurchasing debt, the government buys or sells the composite capital directly. Thus, taking this simpler alternative view, our requirement that tax revenues support government expenditures means that the value of the associated government capital stock must be non-negative in the limit.

To find the value of this capital stock at a point in time, we must evaluate the capital arising out of all previous deficits and surpluses. Let S_ν be the value of capital which results from starting with a one dollar value-equivalent program of composite capital and reinvesting all proceeds from this program, and the resulting proceeds, etc. until time ν. Then, at time T, the value of government capital is

$$\int_0^T S_{T-t}(R_t - X_t)\, \mathrm{d}t. \tag{16}$$

Expressing this in initial dollars, we divide by S_T, the value of an initial investment at time zero compounded by continual reinvestment until time T:

$$\int_0^T \frac{S_{T-t}}{S_T}(R_t - X_t)\, \mathrm{d}t. \tag{17}$$

The term (S_{T-t}/S_T) may be thought of as the discount factor applied to time t deficits.

Given an infinite horizon, the stream of revenues $\{R_t\}$ can support the government expenditures $\{X_t\}$ if the limit of the value in (17) is non-negative:

$$\lim_{T \to \infty} \int_0^T \frac{S_{T-t}}{S_t}(R_t - X_t)\, \mathrm{d}t \geqq 0 \tag{18}$$

which, assuming each limit is finite, implies that

$$\lim_{T \to \infty} \int_0^T \frac{S_{T-t}}{S_T} R_t\, \mathrm{d}t \geqq \lim_{T \to \infty} \int_0^T \frac{S_{T-t}}{S_T} X_t\, \mathrm{d}t. \tag{19}$$

Thus, in terms of government expenditures, which can be supported, the stream $\{R_t\}$ dominates those coming from another value-equivalent program, $\{R_t^*\}$, if and only if

$$\lim_{T \to \infty} \int_0^T \frac{S_{T-t}}{S_T} R_t\, \mathrm{d}t \geqq \lim_{T \to \infty} \int_0^T \frac{S_{T-t}}{S_T} R_t^*\, \mathrm{d}t. \tag{20}$$

Let B_t be the gross return *after* reinvestment from the value-equivalent program which generates R_t; that is [from (14)]:

$$B_t = r + R_t = A_t - D_t \qquad (21)$$

and define B_t^* in the corresponding way. Then condition (20) may be rewritten:

$$\lim_{T \to \infty} \int_0^T \frac{S_{T-t}}{S_T} B_t \, dt \geq \lim_{T \to \infty} \int_0^T \frac{S_{T-t}}{S_T} B_t^* \, dt. \qquad (22)$$

To simplify (22) further, we must examine the behavior of S_v. This term describes the value of the composite capital stock which results from an initial investment of one dollar and the reinvestment of all proceeds for a time period equal to v. This process of capital accumulation has the same characteristics as the growth of a population, where the stream of gross returns from the initial asset represents the stream of 'offspring' this investment produces, with the offspring themselves having the same 'fertility' pattern. What happens to the age structure of the population, or capital stock, over time? By the Strong Ergodic Theorem of stable population theory,[17] the age structure approaches a constant as v approaches infinity. A direct corollary is that the capital stock, and hence S_v, grows exponentially at a constant rate for v sufficiently large. Since this growing capital stock is composed solely of assets with a gross internal rate of return, $r/(1-u)$, it too has an internal rate of $r/(1-u)$. Since all proceeds are being reinvested, the exponential growth rate must therefore be $r/(1-u)$, from which it follows that $S_{T-t}/S_T = -\exp[r/(1-u)]t$ as T becomes large Thus, we may rewrite condition (22) as

$$\int_0^\infty \exp\left(-\frac{r}{1-u}t\right) B_t \, dt \gtreqless \int_0^\infty \exp\left(-\frac{r}{1-u}t\right) B_t^* \, dt. \qquad (23)$$

That is, one value-equivalent program is preferred to another if the present value of its total (public plus private) consumption is higher when discounted at the internal rate of return on society's composite capital.

Now suppose the gross internal rate of return on every asset, and hence every value-equivalent program, is the same. Then, since the composite capital good is simply a combination of such assets, it must also have this same internal rate of return. It follows that this rate of return is $r/(1-u)$, and that all assets have an effective tax rate of u. Therefore, the present value of the streams $\{B_t\}$ and $\{B_t^*\}$ discounted at $r/(1-u)$, must equal unity. Thus, from (23) it is evident that no reallocation of investment will increase government revenues and the tax system may be deemed 'neutral' when production is efficient. Without making any reference to the way in which

[17] See Golubitsky et al. (1975).

the tax system imposes these effective tax rates, we have shown that when debt is present the results of the previous section apply. It is completely irrelevant whether the rate u results for a particular asset from a statutory tax rate higher than u coupled with accelerated depreciation or an investment tax credit, or a lower tax rate with allowances which fall short of economic depreciation. The reason is that, though firms discount after-tax flows at rate r, they behave *as if* they were discounting total flows at $r/(1-u)$, which for this problem (given the qualifications noted above) is the applicable social discount rate.

To summarize the results of this section, we have shown that, regardless of the particular tax structure and the particular types of capital assets which are purchased by investors, the value placed by the government and, *a fortiori*, the social value of different marginal value-equivalent investment projects between which investors are indifferent will be the same if the gross internal rates of return on all such assets are the same. This in turn requires that the effective tax rates on all such investments be equal.

6. Conclusions

Using a framework suggested by difficulties encountered in comparing previous claims about what kind of tax system is neutral, we have analyzed the question of investment tax neutrality. Our results suggest that only the approach which requires effective rates of tax to be the same for different investments can be considered useful as a rule of thumb, and that it may be a sensible approach to take when government debt is available, given the difficulty of solving the full optimal tax problem for the relevant set of constraints on government activity.

References

Arrow, K., 1966, Discounting and public investment criteria, in: A. Kneese and S. Smith, eds., Water research (Resources for the Future, Baltimore).

Atkinson, A. and A. Sandmo, 1980, Welfare implications of the taxation of savings, Economic Journal 90, 529–549.

Auerbach, A., 1978, Neutrality and the corporate tax, Harvard Institute of Economic Research Discussion Paper, no. 657.

Auerbach, A., 1979a Inflation and the choice of asset life, Jorunal of Political Economy 87, 621–638.

Auerbach, A., 1979b, The optimal taxation of heterogeneous capital, Quarterly Journal of Economics 93, 589–612.

Auerbach, A., 1981a, A note on the efficient design of investment incentives, Economic Journal 91, 217–223.

Auerbach, A., 1981b, Inflation and the tax treatment of firm behavior, American Economic Review 71, 419–423.

Auerbach, A. and D. Jorgenson, 1980, Inflation-proof depreciation of assets, Harvard Business Review 58, 113–118.

Black, J., 1959, Investment allowances, initial allowances and cheap loans as means of encouraging investment, Review of Economic Studies 27, 44–49.

Boadway, R., 1978, Investment incentives, corporate taxation, and efficiency in the allocation of capital, Economic Journal 88, 470–481.

Bradford, D., 1980, Tax neutrality and the investment tax credit, in: H. Aaron and M. Boskin, eds., The economics of taxation (The Brookings Institution, Washington).

Chase, S., 1962, Tax credits for investment spending, National Tax Journal 15, 32–52.

Diamond, P. and J. Mirrlees, 1971, Optimal taxation and public production: I, American Economic Review 61, 8–27.

Drèze, J., 1974, Discount rates for public investment, Economica 41, 52–61.

Feldstein, M., 1974, Financing in the evaluation of public expenditure, in: W. Smith and J. Culbertson, eds., Public finance and stabilization policy (North-Holland, Amsterdam).

Feldstein, M., 1981, Adjusting depreciation in an inflationary economy: Indexing versus acceleration, National Tax Journal 34, 29–43.

Golubitsky, M., E. Keeler and M. Rothschild, 1975, Convergence of the age structure: Applications of a projective metric, Theoretical Population Biology, 84–93.

Gordon, R. and D. Jorgenson, 1976, The investment tax credit and countercyclical policy, in: O. Eckstein, ed., Parameters and policies in the U.S. economy (North-Holland, Amsterdam).

Harberger, A., 1980, Tax neutrality in investment incentives, in: H. Aaron and M. Boskin, eds., The economics of taxation (The Brookings Institution, Washington).

Jorgenson, D., 1963, Capital theory and investment behavior, American Economic Review 53, 247–259.

Kay, J., 1972, Social discount rates, Journal of Public Economics 1. 359–378.

Kopcke, R., 1981, Inflation, corporate income taxation and the demand for capital assets, Journal of Political Economy 89, 122–131.

Lucas, R., 1976, Econometric policy evaluation: A critique, in: K. Brunner and A. Meltzer, eds., The Phillips curve and labor markets (North-Holland, Amsterdam).

Marglin, S.A., 1963, The social rate of discount and the optimal rate of investment, Quarterly Journal of Economics 77, 95–111.

Musgrave, R., 1959, The theory of public finance (McGraw-Hill, New York).

Sandmo, A., 1974, Investment incentives and the corporate income tax, Journal of Political Economy 82, 287–302.

Sandmo, A. and J. Drèze, 1971, Discount rates for public investment in closed and open economies, Economica 38, 398–412.

Sunley, E., 1973, Towards a more neutral investment tax credit, National Tax Journal 26, 209–220.

Sunley, E., 1976, Tax neutrality between capital services provided by ling-lived and short-lived assets, U.S. Treasury Office of Tax Analysis, Paper no. 10.

Tideman, T.N., 1975, Measuring the cost of capital services, U.S. Treasury Office of Tax Analysis, Paper no. 4.

3
Efficient Design of Investment Incentives

The importance of investment both as a component of output and a cause of business fluctuations has led to government introduction, in the United Kingdom, the United States and many other countries, of a range of tax incentives aimed at stimulating capital accumulation. Because investment goods are durable, and vary with respect to asset life, a critical issue which has generated much discussion in the literature on capital taxation is the relative treatment of long-lived and short-lived assets.[1] Many authors have invoked the concept of 'neutrality' in evaluating different incentive schemes, and in the past two distinct notions of what constitutes a neutral scheme have been advanced. One view is that an investment incentive is neutral if it has the same proportional effect on internal rates of return of different projects.[2] The other approach requires an equiproportional impact on the 'user cost' of different assets.[3] While intuitive arguments can be offered in support of each approach, the prescriptions of one contradict those of the other, and both views are of an *ad hoc* nature not relating directly to any calculation of a social optimum.

In a recent article in this JOURNAL,[4] Robin Boadway has argued that the appropriate requirement for neutrality is that the present value of the returns from an initial investment of £1, using the social discount rate, should be equal for all projects undertaken at the margin. We have few qualifications about this approach itself; although discounting with the social rate of time preference (STP) may be inappropriate in the current context. However, we would take issue with two aspects of Boadway's application of his view of neutrality. The first problem concerns the appropriate definition of the constraint on firm leverage which would arise from the existence of limited liability. We believe Boadway's assumption to be inappropriate, and find that its replacement with what we argue to be the correct one leads to important revisions in evaluating the neutrality of different incentives. Another point we would make is that Boadway's results depend crucially on the absence of both personal taxes and inflation. We argue below that once realistic account has been taken of these important elements of the problem, general results about the neutrality of different incentives can no longer be derived, so that while Boadway's criterion may be appropriate, its application promises to be very difficult.

I am grateful to John Flemming, Robin Boadway and Julian Alworth for comments on earlier drafts.

[1] While discussion has tended to focus on the corporate sector, most incentives, at least in the United States (including the investment tax credit and accelerated depreciation) apply to the unincorporated sector as well. We shall follow the usual approach since most nonresidential investment is done by corporations.

[2] This is the criterion used by Musgrave (1959) and Harberger (1980), among others.

[3] See, for example, Sunley (1973) or Sandmo (1974).

[4] Boadway (1978).

I. NEUTRALITY AND THE DISCOUNT RATE

Applied to the case in which capital of type i, K_i, depreciates exponentially at rate δ_i and output is produced according to a neoclassical production function, $F_i(k_i)$ Boadway's criterion requires that, at the margin

$$PV_i = \int_0^\infty e^{-rt} \frac{\partial F_i}{\partial K_i} e^{-\delta_i t}\, dt \tag{1}$$

be independent of i, where r is the real social discount rate, taken to be the consumption rate of interest. Since all of the results about neutrality depend on the choice of r, an explanation might be appropriate in light of the great controversy which continues to be waged over the appropriate social discount rate.

In general, it is well known that simply discounting the flows from a project with the social rate of time preference (STP) may be inappropriate unless either all such flows are entirely consumed without any reinvestment occurring or the prevailing return to capital in the private sector, the social opportunity cost (SOC), equals the STP. Since neither of these conditions applies in the current context, one might criticise Boadway for his approach.

There are cases in which Boadway's criterion does turn out to be appropriate. As Kay (1972), drawing upon the work of Arrow (1966), has demonstrated, if one assumes that a constant fraction s of all project returns are reinvested at the given SOC, denoted $p(>sr)$, the present value of a project in terms of eventual consumption is:

$$PV_i^* = P_i \frac{p(1-s)}{p-rs}, \tag{2}$$

where PV_i is as defined in equation (1). Thus, equality of PV^* among projects is achieved if and only if equality among the basic PV's is satisfied. However, the assumption that s is independent of project choice, while perhaps accurate for smaller problems of expenditure evaluation, is less appealing when we consider corporate investment as a whole, for it implies that the aggregate time stream of consumption is dependent on the durability of capital.

While we consider this an important issue in itself, further treatment lies beyond the scope of this note. We therefore accept Boadway's criterion for the remainder of our discussion.

II. INTEREST DEDUCTIBILITY AND THE BORROWING CONSTRAINT

In the absence of uncertainty and personal taxes, the ability of corporations to deduct interest payments from taxable income makes debt strictly preferable over equity as a financing method. Clearly, some constraint is required to prevent firms from engaging in infinite borrowing. Boadway assumes that firms are constrained to keep the amount of their outstanding debt A at or below the size of their capital stock:

$$A \leqslant K. \tag{3}$$

That this makes little sense may be seen from the following simple example. Suppose the tax law allows free depreciation of capital,[1] with no other special incentives offered. Then, in equilibrium, the value of new capital goods which cost £1 to produce is £1 to investing firms, while used capital goods of equivalent productive capability must be worth £$(1-u)$, where u is the corporate tax rate, since they do not possess the immediate tax deduction of value £u. Now, consider a new enterprise which purchases £1 of indestructible capital ($\delta = 0$), financing it with the sale of £1 of debt. The firm's equity has value £0, the value of its capital less the value of its debt. One year later, the *value* of the firm's £1 of capital is £$(1-u)$, but it still, according to condition (3), may maintain £1 of debt. The firm's equity is now worth $-$£u, and bankruptcy followed by the formation of a new enterprise would seem in order.

The problem illustrated by the example above arises because the constraint on the firm is phrased in terms of the firm's physical stock of capital, rather than its market value.[2] Boadway's use of the former appears to derive[3] from the coincidence of physical and market value in the case of economic depreciation, a result which holds precisely because the value of depreciation allowances allotted to a capital good relate only to its remaining productivity, and not to its vintage. Since Boadway uses economic depreciation as a source of comparison because it is neutral, the difficulty in interpreting his results is evident. We therefore should like to impose the alternative constraint that debt not exceed in value the project which it finances, and see how this affects the results. To do this, we first develop a method for considering the general case in which firms finance with a given ratio of debt to project value, a special case of which is when this value is unity.[4]

Let ρ be the nominal equity discount rate (equal to r when there are no personal taxes or inflation) and define E_t as the project's rate of cash flow at instant t. The increment to equity arising from the project at time t is:

$$v_t = \int_t^\infty e^{-\rho(s-t)} E_s \, ds. \tag{4}$$

The value to the firm from undertaking a project at time zero, denoted w_0, is the increment to equity value deriving from future receipts, v_0, plus the receipts from the initial flotation of debt, A_0. To derive an expression for this sum, we first differentiate (4) with respect to time, getting:

$$\rho v_t = E_t + \dot{v}_t. \tag{5}$$

---

[1] Known as 'expensing' in the United States.

[2] Alworth (1979), in criticising Boadway's approach, has suggested as a third alternative for the constraint on debt the amount the firm would realise by selling its assets, taking account of deferred capital gains taxes on such a sale. This value would be lower than the firm's market value unless the firm actually would choose to sell its assets, which does not appear to be the usual case. Thus, Alworth's restriction will normally result in the firm's equity having a positive value. Such a constraint is therefore not related to the limited liability of the firm as such, but might represent the convention of lending institutions who look at balance sheets rather than market value.

[3] Boadway (1978), page 473, footnote 3.

[4] A complete version of the analysis which follows appears in Auerbach (1979b).

Letting x_t be the rate of cash flow at time t ignoring increments in the stock of debt, A_t, and interest payments net of tax, (5) becomes:

$$\rho v_t = x_t + \dot{A}_t - r^G(1-u)A_t + \dot{v}_t, \tag{6}$$

where r^G is the gross nominal interest rate (equal to r when there are no personal taxes or inflation associated with the project). Letting b be the ratio of the value of debt at time t to the value of debt + equity,[1] we may rewrite (6) as:

$$i(v_t + A_t) = x_t + (v_t + A_t), \tag{7}$$

where

$$i = br^G(1-u) + (1-b)\rho \tag{8}$$

is a weighted average cost of capital. Under the usual convergence assumption, (7) yields:

$$w_0 = \int_0^\infty e^{-it} x_t \, dt. \tag{9}$$

Since x_t does not depend on the fraction b, we may easily derive the 'user cost' of capital for the firm as a function of b by maximising w_0 less the initial cost of investment goods, for i given, and then evaluate the expression we obtain for different assumptions about b, and hence i.

Table 1 presents the cost of capital for some of the incentive schemes analysed by Boadway, whose own results are offered for comparison in column 5. In all cases, economic depreciation based on historic cost is assumed. Column 3 presents results for the general case in which b is arbitrary and the rate of inflation π (assumed by Boadway to be zero) may be positive,[2] while those in column 4 derive from the assumptions of no inflation ($\pi = 0$) and full debt finance at the margin ($b = 1$). For the general case in column 3, the cost of capital consists of three terms, one relating to the firm's real discount rate, $(i - \pi)$, one relating to depreciation, δ, and a third which represents the loss in real value of depreciation allowances due to inflation.[3] In all cases presented, the cost of capital in column 4 exceeds that in column 5 by the value of the incentive as a fraction of total investment cost multiplied by the term $ru/(1-u)$. This result has a straightforward explanation. For example, suppose an investment tax credit of value σ is given. The value of capital drops immediately by σ after the credit is taken. Under the requirement that $A = W$ rather than $A = K$ the amount of bonds must drop by the same fraction, reducing the tax deduction by $r\sigma$, which means a loss in before tax pounds of $r\sigma u/(1-u)$. Of course, if the incentive accrues over time, as with accelerated depreciation, no

---

[1] It should be emphasised here that b is employed as the fraction of debt used in financing a marginal project, not the ratio of debt to market value for the firm as a whole. For example, imagine Coca-Cola considering the addition of a new bottling plant. The management would compare the cost of the plant with the increment to wealth the plant would generate.

[2] The complete derivation of these results is omitted for the sake of brevity. With an investment allowance, firms choose K_t at each point in time to maximise:

$$\int_0^\infty e^{-it}\left[(1-u)e^{\pi t}F(K_t) - e^{\pi t}(1-u\theta)(\dot{K}_t + \delta K_t) + u\int_{-\infty}^t (\dot{K}_s + \delta K_s)\delta e^{-\delta(t-s)}ds\right]dt.$$

The Euler condition for this problem yields the result in Table 1. The other results follow from similar maximisation problems.

[3] See Auerbach (1979a) for further interpretation of this 'inflation tax' on depreciation.

Table 1

Cost of Capital Under Different Regimes

(1) Type of Incentive	(2) Description	(3) b, π unspecified	(4) $b = 1$, $\pi = 0$	(5) $b = K/W$, $\pi = 0$
Investment allowance	Deduction of a fraction θ of gross investment from taxable income	$(i-\pi)\left(\dfrac{1-u\theta}{1-u}\right)$ $+\pi\left(\dfrac{u}{1-u}\right)\left(\dfrac{\delta}{i+\delta}\right)$ $+\delta\left(1-\dfrac{u\theta}{1-u}\right)$	$r(1-u\theta)+\delta\left(1-\dfrac{u\theta}{1-u}\right)$	$r\left(1-\dfrac{u\theta}{1-u}\right)+\delta\left(1-\dfrac{u\theta}{1-u}\right)$
Initial allowance	Deduction of a fraction ϕ of gross investment with depreciation applied to a fraction $(1-\phi)$	$(i-\pi)\left(\dfrac{1-u\phi}{1-u}\right)+\delta$ $+\pi\left(\dfrac{u}{1-u}\right)\left(\dfrac{\delta}{i+\delta}\right)(1-\phi)$	$r(1-u\phi)+\delta$	$r\left(1-\dfrac{u\phi}{1-u}\right)+\delta$
Investment tax credit (gross)	Credit of a fraction σ of gross investment, with entire basis subject to depreciation	Same as investment allowance for $\sigma = u\theta$		
Investment tax credit (gross) with basis adjustment	Credit of a fraction σ of gross investment with $(1-\sigma)$, of initial basis subject to depreciation	$(i-\pi)\left(\dfrac{1-\sigma}{1-u}\right)+\delta(1-\sigma)$ $+\pi\left(\dfrac{u}{1-u}\right)\left(\dfrac{\delta}{i+\delta}\right)(1-\sigma)$	$r(1-\sigma)+\delta(1-\sigma)$	$r\left(1-\dfrac{\sigma}{1-u}\right)+\delta(1-\sigma)$
Investment tax credit (net)	Credit of a fraction β on net investment, with entire basis subject to depreciation	$(i-\pi)\left(\dfrac{1-\beta}{1-u}\right)+\delta$ $+\pi\left(\dfrac{u}{1-u}\right)\left(\dfrac{\delta}{i+\delta}\right)$	$r(1-\beta)+\delta$	$r\left(1-\dfrac{\beta}{1-u}\right)+\delta$
Economic depreciation		$(i-\pi)\left(\dfrac{1}{1-u}\right)+\delta$ $+\pi\left(\dfrac{u}{1-u}\right)\left(\dfrac{\delta}{i+\delta}\right)$	$r+\delta$	$r+\delta$

equally simple comparison is likely to result and, presumably, δ will enter into the calculation. Note also that in the curious but feasible event that the incentive took a form which made old capital more attractive than new capital (e.g., a 'scrapping credit' paid upon an asset's reaching the end of its useful life) W would exceed K and the cost of capital would be lower under the restriction that $A \leqslant W$.

Returning to the issue of neutrality, an incentive is neutral (from equation (1) and the equality of $\partial F / \partial K$ and the cost of capital, c, in equilibrium) if

$$c = k(r+\delta), \qquad (10)$$

where k is a constant. This criterion is satisfied by the gross ITC with basis adjustment under our assumptions, found by Boadway to favour long-lived investments. Investment Allowances and the gross ITC without basis adjustment favour short-lived investment using our calculations, contrary to Boadway's certification of neutrality.

III. PERSONAL TAXES

All of the above discussion is really beside the point, in a way, since few would argue that a realistic analysis can be conducted while ignoring potentially high rates of inflation and personal taxation. Even maintaining Boadway's assumptions that $b = 1$ and $\pi = 0$, economic depreciation is not neutral with personal taxes present. We get the following expression for the cost of capital from the last entry in column 3 of Table 1:

$$c = r^G + \delta. \qquad (11)$$

Letting t_p be the personal tax rate on interest income, so that[1]

$$r = r^G(1 - t_p) \qquad (12)$$

(11) becomes

$$c = r\left(\frac{1}{1 - t_p}\right) + \delta \qquad (13)$$

which implies that economic depreciation is neutral if and only if $t_p = 0$.

If we were to consider the more general problem of a firm using mixed finance, we would first need to explain the existence of an interior solution to the choice between debt and equity. One solution would be to assume the existence of some constraint that b not exceed some value b^* between 0 and 1. In such a case, if we still maintain the assumption that $\pi = 0$, the cost of capital would be:

$$c = b^* r^G + (1 - b^*) \frac{\rho}{1 - u} + \delta. \qquad (14)$$

Letting t_e be the effective marginal tax rate on equity income,[1] so that

$$r = \rho(1 - t_e) \qquad (15)$$

---

[1] Presumably, some value between the tax rate on dividends and the accrual-equivalent of the capital gains tax rate, although I argue in Auerbach (1979b) that it should be the latter value, regardless of payout rate.

the cost of capital in (11) may be written:

$$c = r\left[\frac{b^*}{1-t_p} + \frac{(1-b^*)}{(1-u)(1-t_e)}\right] + \delta \tag{16}$$

which implies that neutrality results if and only if $t_p = t_e = u = 0$. An alternative assumption which would potentially lead to an interior solution for b would be the existence of different classes of individuals with different tax rates. However, in such a situation, individuals would have different rates of discount, and the neutrality criterion would no longer be well-defined.

Even with all individuals possessing the same discount rate, the results of this section indicate the non-neutralities introduced by personal taxes to an otherwise neutral corporate tax structure. Moreover, we have not even considered the important effects of inflation that are due to the tax system not being indexed. Regaining neutrality through incentive design would likely require a very complex relationship between asset life and the size of the incentive.

IV. CONCLUSION

We have argued that even if Boadway's criterion for judging investment incentives is an appropriate one, his application of it to the analysis of investment incentives must be adjusted to include a more natural specification of the borrowing constraint faced by corporations. Moreover, the specification of neutral incentives becomes much more complicated once realistic allowance is made for the presence of inflation and personal taxes.

REFERENCES

Alworth, J. S. (1979). 'Investment incentives, corporate taxation and efficiency in the allocation of capital — a comment.' ECONOMIC JOURNAL, vol. 89 (September).
Arrow, K. J. (1966). 'Discounting and public investment criteria.' In *Water Research* (ed. Kneese and Smith), pp. 13–32. Baltimore: Resources for the Future.
Auerbach, A. J. (1979a). 'Inflation and the choice of asset life.' *Journal of Political Economy*, vol. 87 (June), pp. 621–38.
—— (1979b). 'Wealth maximization and the cost of capital.' *Quarterly Journal of Economics*, vol. 93 (August), pp. 433–46.
Boadway, R. (1978). 'Investment incentives, corporate taxation, and the efficiency of capital.' ECONOMIC JOURNAL, vol. 88 (September), pp. 470–81.
Harberger, A. C. (1980). 'Tax neutrality in investment incentives.' In *The Economics of Taxation* (ed. Aaron and Boskin). Washington: The Brookings Institution.
Kay, J. A. (1972). 'Social discount rates.' *Journal of Public Economics*, vol. 1 (November), pp. 359–78.
Musgrave, R. A. (1959). *The Theory of Public Finance*. New York: McGraw-Hill.
Sandmo, A. (1974). 'Investment incentives and the corporate tax.' *Journal of Political Economy*, vol. 82 (March–April), pp. 387–402.
Sunley, E. M. (1973). 'Towards a more neutral investment tax credit.' *National Tax Journal*, vol. 26 (June), pp. 209–20.

___ PART II
TAXATION AND
CORPORATE FINANCE

The United States has what is often referred to as a "classical" system of taxing corporate and personal income. A corporation is taxed on its income, independent of the identity of its shareholders. These shareholders, in turn, are taxed on distributions from the firm (dividends) and capital gains realized on the sale of shares, regardless of the income earned by the corporation itself or the taxes it pays. Corporations and their owners are also treated independently in the national income accounts. Here, the concept of "personal income" includes in the income attributed to individuals only the dividends and capital gains actually realized during the year, rather than all income earned by corporations.

However, if one views the corporation as a conduit for transmitting investment earnings to individual stockholders, then taxes at both corporate and personal levels must be considered together to gain an impression of the overall impact of the tax system. Analyses of this sort typically lead to a number of results. First, it is in the interest of stockholders for corporations to retain earnings rather than pay dividends, since by retaining they convert earnings into nontaxed or (if actually realized) lightly taxed capital gains at the personal level, rather than fully taxed dividends. Second, if dividends are paid, there is a double tax on corporate earnings, since such dividends come from earnings already taxed at the corporate rate, and are themselves taxable at the individual level. Finally, to the extent that risk permits, debt financing should be used by corporations, since interest payments are deductible at the corporate level.

Yet U.S. corporations distribute perhaps half of their earnings as dividends, and use debt financing less frequently than might be expected from the double-taxation argument. The two chapters in Part II offer a possible explanation for this.

The assumption that dividends are doubly taxed is challenged in "Share Valuation and Corporate Equity Policy." If double taxation is a myth, corporations would appear to have less reason to choose to retain earnings rather than to distribute them. The mechanism by which this indifference comes about is a discount in the valuation of new investment by the stock market: a dollar of new investment causes the firm's market value to increase by less than a dollar. Therefore,

59

the tax gain from avoiding the payment of dividends is offset. While people still pay taxes on dividends when they receive them, these extra tax payments are defrayed by the premium representing the difference between each dollar received and its value to the stockholder if it had been retained by the corporation. This "new view" also helps to explain the coexistence of debt and equity financing, since it suggests that all equity income is effectively taxed at capital gains rates at the personal level, regardless of the form the income takes.

A second part of the story involves individuals in different tax brackets, one of the issues considered in "Wealth Maximization and the Cost of Capital." Given that the U.S. tax system is progressive, and that some asset holders are actually endowed with a zero tax rate on income through tax exempt status, it is possible for corporations to be indifferent between debt and equity financing if constraints are placed on individual tax arbitrage behavior. This result, in its basic form, is Miller's ("Debt and Taxes," *Journal of Finance* 32 [May 1977], 261-275), but is more plausible when combined with the "new view" of equity taxation. It can be extended to the more general case where asset returns are risky, as described in Auerbach and King, "Taxation, Portfolio Choice and Debt-Equity Ratios: A General Equilibrium Model," *Quarterly Journal of Economics* 98, forthcoming, and Auerbach, "Taxes, Firm Financial Policy and the Cost of Capital: An Empirical Analysis," *Journal of Public Economics*, forthcoming. The general argument is very simple. Though equity income faces the corporate tax and interest income does not, equity income is taxed at a lower rate at the personal level. Either some equity income (under the traditional view) or all equity income (under the new view) receives preferential capital gains treatment. For low-bracket investors, the advantage is clearly with debt. For investors in tax brackets somewhat above the corporate rate, the advantage switches to equity. Thus, the latter will hold equity, the former debt. Either group could do better by increasing their holdings of the pre-ferred security by holding negative quantities of the other, so un-limited arbitrage behavior of this kind must be ruled out, as in practice it is. It is not possible, for example, for individuals to buy equity completely on margin. Similarly, there are restrictions on short sales of equity.

These results have important implications for the choice of tax policies to stimulate investment. In particular, a cut in the tax rate on dividends would not increase the incentive to invest, because dividend taxes do not directly influence the effective tax rate on equity income. Furthermore, schemes to "integrate" personal and corporate taxes by, in effect, removing taxes on dividends and capital gains and replacing the corporate tax with an individual tax on corporate source

income, would result in a large windfall for the owners of existing shares with conceivably little additional economic effect. (See the discussion in Auerbach, "Tax Integration and the 'New View' of the Corporate Tax: A 1980s Perspective," *Proceedings of the National Tax Association-Tax Institute of America* [1981], 21-27.)

4

Share Valuation and Corporate Equity Policy

1. Introduction

In recent years, many contributions have appeared which examine the effects of corporate and personal taxation on firm financial policy.[1] One important aspect of the problem in the U.S. and certain other countries is the preferential tax treatment accorded capital gains, which are taxed upon realization, and then only at a rate that is substantially below that on regular capital income.[2] This provision has led Stiglitz (1973) and others to conclude that, in the absence of uncertainty, corporations should retain earnings as long as possible, with the eventual recovery of profits by shareholders taking the form of capital gains. Nevertheless, dividends remain an important method of transmitting corporate profits, and a framework capable of explaining such behavior is needed. The chief aim of this paper is to present and develop such a model.

The author would like to thank Martin Feldstein, John Flemming, Jerry Green, and Lawrence Summers for discussions and helpful comments on previous drafts, and Anthony Atkinson for many useful suggestions, which include the ingenious diagram presented in this paper.

[1]See, for example, Gordon (1962), Farrar and Selwyn (1967), Pye (1972), Stapleton (1972), Stiglitz (1973, 1976) and King (1974).

[2]In the U.S., long-term capital gains are generally taxed at 50% of the rate on distributions, there existing various provisions which may make the rate higher or lower for particular taxpayers.

An issue related to the firm financial decision is the proper criterion for new investment. Tobin (1969) has argued that firms will have an incentive to invest when the market price of their equity is greater than the reproduction cost of the capital which the equity represents.

In the present paper we explore once more the determinants of corporate equity policy and investment. Our economy consists of a large number of corporations which finance their capital investments solely through equity. These corporations behave in a perfectly competitive manner. Individuals save by purchasing shares of stock. The stock's value increases to reflect the retention of corporate earnings. We assume that all individuals have the same preferences and face the same marginal tax rates, and that, in addition to facing the same corporate tax rate, corporations face the same set of production possibilities.

Absent from the analysis is an important aspect of corporate finance, the issuance of debt. While, in reality, firms would generally find it advantageous to achieve a certain degree of leverage, there are various reasons, including legal restrictions and the possibility of bankruptcy, why firms would wish to maintain corporate equity at a certain level in their marginal financing. In the same vein, we have excluded the government and noncorporate sectors as alternative vehicles for personal saving.

There are a few remaining assumptions we desire to make which will rule out behavior that is either illegal or implausible. We assume that firms cannot buy back their own shares. It is evident that such a policy strictly dominates the issuance of dividends, since the sole difference between the two policies is the rate at which the personal receipts are taxed. However, share repurchases have historically been extremely small relative to regular dividend distributions in the U.S.,[3] perhaps, in part, because of Section 302 of the Internal Revenue Code which provides for the taxation at the regular personal tax rate of repurchases deemed to be in lieu of dividends.[4] In the same spirit, we rule out any systematic interfirm share purchases using undistributed funds. Suppose, for the moment, that firms could pass through share earnings without additional corporate taxation. Then, by buying each other's shares, two firms could effectively circumvent the share repurchase prohibition. Actually, the U.S. tax code exempts only 85% of dividends received by corporations, and taxes capital gains at the corporate level. Thus, ignoring questions of legality, the superiority of interfirm shares purchases over dividends would depend on the average holding time of such shares. Regardless of the outcome of this calculation, it seems unrealistic to consider interfirm investment as more than a negligible use for corporate funds.

The partial taxation of firm-held shares could, in principle, be alleviated completely by outright acquisition of other firms. However, antitrust laws

---

[3] Relevant statistics are cited in Auerbach (1979).
[4] In the U.K., repurchases are prohibited outright.

and other legal constraints pose barriers to such activity and, as in the case of simple investment in other firms' shares, it is not very plausible as a marginal alternative.

The above simplifications imply that firms may hold two types of assets: physical capital and liquid stocks which yield no physical return. If prices were subject to change or there were costs associated with shifts in production, there would be valid reasons for maintaining liquidity in the form of inventories. While we do not rule out such holdings in our model, we show in the Appendix that they will never be held by firms. Thus, all firm receipts, coming from profits and the sale of new shares, will either be distributed as dividends or retained and reinvested in new capital. Our results indicate that the superiority of capital gains over dividends as a method of profit distribution depends on the valuation of a share of stock. We find that, in a steady state, stock may be sufficiently undervalued so that dividends become an attractive method of distribution. With respect to the corporation's investment criterion, we concur that firms will finance investment through the sale of new shares only when share price exceeds reproduction cost. However, reinvestment of retained earnings will occur as long as share price exceeds a particular level which is strictly less than reproduction cost.

The share price which obtains in equilibrium varies in response to changes in the various rates of taxation. This has important implications for the return earned by investors, as well as the long-run capital intensity of the economy.

We present our model more explicitly in the following section. In section 3 we offer an analysis of how share prices may fall below reproduction cost in a dynamic economy. In section 4 we use comparative statics to analyze the effects that changes in different tax rates may have on the capital–labor ratio, return to investors, and share valuation, and illustrate these results diagrammatically with a Cobb–Douglas example. A few concluding comments appear in the final section.

2. The model

We examine the characteristics of a steady state in a one-sector non-monetary growth model with overlapping generations of individuals. We assume there is no inflation, and take output as numeraire. This output may be used as capital or consumed, but, once it is put in place as capital it loses its fungibility and may not be consumed subsequently. Individuals live for two periods, and the population grows at rate n. At the end of each period, members of the younger generation save in the form of shares. There are no bequests, so that dividends received in the second period are consumed immediately, as are the receipts from the sale of all shares held. The value of

a firm is the reproduction cost of the capital it holds, multiplied by Tobin's 'q', the ratio of share value to replacement cost. For simplicity, we always measure shares in units of capital, so that each share has price q. Thus, if firms increase their value by acquiring more capital, the number of shares outstanding, rather than the price per share, will increase. The process can be seen as a stock dividend in which new shares are given to each current stockholder in such a way as to maintain the amount of capital owned by each share. This should not be confused with the outside sale of new shares.

Labor supply per capita is taken to be fixed, and labor units are set so that each worker supplies one unit of labor.

An important issue is the use to which tax receipts are put. One can imagine several possibilities, including transfers to either or both generations, the purchase of public goods, or the investment in public projects.[5] We assume for the sake of simplicity that tax receipts are spent by the government on items which do not affect individual decisions (e.g. military expenditures).

From the assumption of utility maximization, we may derive individual demand functions for first and second period consumption. Letting r be the after-tax return to savers, second period consumption and saving are related by

$$c_2 = (1 + r)s \tag{1}$$

so that we may derive the savings function

$$s = s(r, y) \tag{2}$$

where y is first period labor income.

Production in each firm is governed by the constant returns to scale relation

$$x = f(k), \qquad f' > 0; \ f'' < 0, \tag{3}$$

where k is the firm's capital–labor ratio. Since all firms are identical and follow the same policies, k is also the economy-wide capital–labor ratio.

Savers buy shares, each representing one unit of capital, at price q. Thus, at any time the economy's capital stock is

$$K_t = (s/q)N_t^2 \tag{4}$$

where N_t^2 is the population of the older generation at time t. Letting N_t^1 be

---

[5]Feldstein (1974) has demonstrated how the use to which government tax receipts are put may influence the long-run incidence of such taxes.

the population of the younger generation, and hence the supply of labor to the economy, we know that $N_t^1/N_t^2 = (1+n)$, so that

$$k = s[q(1+n)]^{-1}. \tag{5}$$

There are three taxes of concern in our analysis: the corporate tax rate, τ, assessed immediately on all firm profits; the personal tax rate, θ, on dividends; and the capital gains tax, c, applicable to gains realized on the sale of shares.[6] We assume that all taxes are between zero and unity, and that c is less than θ. We also assume that wages are deductible from corporate profits for tax purposes; perfect competition ensures that firms will equate the marginal product of labor, gross of corporate taxes, with the wage rate. Thus, first period per capita income is

$$y = f - kf'. \tag{6}$$

We turn now to the determination of firm equity policy. The firm's objective is to maximize the return of its current stockholders. If $q > 1$, firms may sell new shares, purchase capital, and realize a gain of $(q-1)$ per share sold, which may then be distributed to current stockholders or reinvested. If $q < 1$, firms would lose on each such sale. If $q = 1$, firms are indifferent between selling and not selling new shares, since no gain or loss occurs. Thus, firms may be observed offering new shares only if $q \geq 1$. Since firms would attempt to sell an infinite number of shares were $q > 1$, it must also be true that $q \leq 1$. Therefore, firms will offer new shares only if $q = 1$, and there will never be a net gain or loss from such sales on the part of current stockholders. Thus, the net return per share, after corporate taxes, is simply the net marginal product of capital, $f'(1-\tau)$. Since shares cost q, the rate of return on savings at the corporate level is

$$\pi = f'(1-\tau)/q. \tag{7}$$

This return may be either retained and reinvested or distributed as a dividend. If the latter occurs, the return is taxed at rate θ, so that the rate of return to savings is

$$r_D = f'(1-\tau)(1-\theta)/q. \tag{8}$$

If the profits π are reinvested, they may buy $f'(1-\tau)/q$ units of capital, each having a share value of q. Thus, the increase in share value, or capital gain,

---

[6]Since all gains are realized in the period of accrual, there is no deferral advantage in taking capital gains.

resulting, would be $f'(1-\tau)$. After capital gains taxation upon the sale of shares, this yields a return to savings of

$$r_R = f'(1-\tau)(1-c). \tag{9}$$

From the fact that firms seek to maximize r, it follows that they will prefer dividends, retentions, or be indifferent, according to whether q is less than, greater than, or equal to q_D, where

$$q_D = (1-\theta)/(1-c). \tag{10}$$

Since $q_D < 1$, firms in our model will never distribute dividends and issue new shares simultaneously. When q is between q_D and unity, firms will not offer new shares to finance investment. However, they will reinvest all of their profits in new capital. Thus, the condition that q be at least one is sufficient, but not necessary, for the existence of new investment. It is necessary only with respect to the offering of new shares.

To close our model we require that the stock market clear in every period. This means that shares of stock outstanding must grow at the same rate as the population, n. Additions to stock come from reinvestment of retained earnings and the sale of new shares. Thus, defining δ as the ratio of new issues to existing shares and γ as the fraction of earnings distributed as dividends, the stock market equilibrium is described by the condition

$$n = f'(1-\tau)(1-\gamma)+\delta. \tag{11}$$

It follows from (11) that there will be dividends in equilibrium if and only if $f'(1-\tau) > n$, and new share issues if and only if $f'(1-\tau) < n$. It is also apparent that q may never be less than q_D in a steady state. If it were, firms would offer no new shares and retain no earnings, i.e. $\delta = 0$ and $\gamma = 1$. Since n is positive, this violates condition (11). The requirement that $q \geq q_D$ implies, in turn, that retentions will be at least as attractive as dividends, so that $r = r_R$. Using these restrictions, and the various equations of this section, we may now conveniently summarize the model we are using. The core of the model consists of four equations in six unknowns, r, k, y, q, δ, and γ:

$$k = s(r,y)[q(1+n)]^{-1}, \tag{12.1}$$

$$r = f'(1-\tau)(1-c), \tag{12.2}$$

$$y = f - kf', \tag{12.3}$$

$$n = f'(1-\tau)(1-\gamma)+\delta. \tag{12.4}$$

The remaining specification depends on the equity regime that applies. There

are three regimes which are feasible, depending of the value of q. For each, there are additional conditions on q, δ, and γ. The regimes, and their corresponding conditions, are presented in table 1.

Table 1

Equity policy regimes.

Dividends	New shares	Conditions
Yes	no	$q = q_D$ $\gamma > 0$ $\delta = 0$
No	yes	$q = 1$ $\gamma = 0$ $\delta > 0$
No	no	$q_D \leqq q \leqq 1$ $\gamma = 0$ $\delta = 0$

For each regime we have two additional equations in the unknowns q, δ and γ which allow us to reduce the number of unknowns in (12) to four, plus an inequality constraint which must be satisfied by the resulting solution to (12). For example, for an equilibrium with dividends to occur, the value of γ arrived at by solving (12) for $q = q_D$ and $\delta = 0$ must be non-negative.

Without characterizing the savings and production functions, we are unable to demonstrate the existence of a unique equilibrium in a particular regime for given values of n, τ, θ, and c.[7]

3. How can stock become undervalued?

We have described above the steady-state behavior of an economy in which share prices may be below unity, so that ownership of capital may be valued at less than the reproduction cost of the capital itself. By what mechanism can this undervaluation come about?

The dynamics of adjustment for the general case would be extremely difficult to model. However, insight into the problem may be gained by examining the simple case in which per capita savings is fixed.

Consider an economy 'just starting up' in which individuals of the first generation buy s units of capital each. At the end of the next period the stockholders not only have the original s units of capital to sell, but also have profits of $sf'(1 - \tau)$. As long as price per share remains at one, the return will be greater from reinvesting these profits in new capital, rather

[7]Theoretically, it might be possible for multiple equilibria to exist within a particular regime, or for equilibria to exist in more than one regime. For the Cobb–Douglas example presented below, there exists a unique equilibrium for each set of tax values.

than taking dividends. Suppose all of the profits are reinvested. Then the stock of capital must grow by a factor of $f'(1-\tau)$, while the demand for capital by the next generation is $(1+n)$ times that of the current owners. If n exceeds $f'(1-\tau)$, all share sales will be accommodated and new shares will be issued to satisfy any remaining demand. But if $n < f'(1-\tau)$, not all shares can be sold. The excess supply of shares will drive down their price. As long as the price remains above $(1-\theta)/(1-c)$, it will still be advantageous to the older generation to reinvest and absorb the lower value of the stock than distribute dividends. If q falls to q_D, current stock owners will be indifferent between retentions and dividends. The price can fall no more, since this would eliminate all reinvestment and, as long as n is positive, there would be an excess demand for shares.

If $q < 1$, then the new generation is able to buy more than one dollar of capital per dollar of savings. Thus, the capital–labor ratio in the following period will be higher, and f' will be lower. If $f'(1-\tau)$ declines to n, then all profits can be reinvested and shares can be sold to the third generation at the price that cleared the market in the previous period, since shares and savings will have grown at the same rate. If $f'(1-\tau)$ remains above n, full reinvestment will lead to an excess supply of shares at that price, and q must fall again. If the new market-clearing price is above $(1-\theta)/(1-c)$, this policy remains superior to dividend payouts. However, if the price reaches q_D, firms will choose to reinvest only a portion of their earnings, and offer dividends.

This process would continue over time. Eventually, one of two outcomes would have to occur. If q declines to $(1-\theta)/(1-c)$ before $f'(1-\tau)$ declines to n, then dividends will be paid and $[f'(1-\tau)-n]$ will remain positive. If $f'(1-\tau)$ reaches n and q exceeds $(1-\theta)/(1-c)$, then q will stop falling and there will be no dividends paid in equilibrium.

4. Effects of tax rate changes

We now examine the general equilibrium effects that changes in the tax rates τ, c, and θ have on the steady-state values of k, the capital–labor ratio, r, the return to savings, and q, the share price of a unit of firm-held capital, for each of the three regimes discussed above. The results are listed in table 2. For ease of exposition, we totally differentiate each system with respect to $\tilde{\tau} = (1-\tau)$, $\tilde{\theta} = (1-\theta)$, and $\tilde{c} = (1-c)$, rather than the taxes themselves. Note that the elasticity of any parameter i with respect to any tax j, η_{ij}, has the opposite sign from the elasticity of i with respect to $\tilde{j}$. Therefore, we present the values of $-\eta_{ij}$ in the table.

Many of the results depend on the values of η_{sr}, $[1-(S_K/\sigma)\eta_{sy}]$ and Δ (defined in table 2). The first is the uncompensated or 'total' supply elasticity of personal savings with respect to the rate of return. In theory, η_{sr} may be positive or negative. Econometric research has traditionally found η_{sr} to be

Table 2

Tax change effects.[a]

Elasticity	Regime		
	Retained earnings + new shares	Retained earnings only	Retained earnings + dividends
$-\eta_{k\bar{\imath}}$	$-\dfrac{1}{\Delta}\eta_{sr}$	$-\dfrac{\sigma}{S_L}$	$-\dfrac{1}{\Delta}\eta_{sr}$
$-\eta_{r\bar{\imath}}$	$-\dfrac{1}{\Delta}\left(1-\dfrac{S_K}{\sigma}\eta_{sy}\right)$	0	$-\dfrac{1}{\Delta}\left(1-\dfrac{S_K}{\sigma}\eta_{sy}\right)$
$-\eta_{q\bar{\imath}}$	0	$\dfrac{\sigma}{S_L}\left(1-\dfrac{S_K}{\sigma}\eta_{sy}\right)$	0
$-\eta_{k\bar{c}}$	$-\dfrac{1}{\Delta}\eta_{sr}$	0	$-\dfrac{1}{\Delta}(\eta_{sr}+1)$
$-\eta_{r\bar{c}}$	$-\dfrac{1}{\Delta}\left(1-\dfrac{S_K}{\sigma}\eta_{sy}\right)$	-1	$-\dfrac{1}{\Delta}\left(1-\dfrac{S_K}{\sigma}\eta_{sy}-\dfrac{S_L}{\sigma}\right)$
$-\eta_{q\bar{c}}$	0	$-\eta_{sr}$	1
$-\eta_{k\theta}$	0	0	$\dfrac{1}{\Delta}$
$-\eta_{r\theta}$	0	0	$-\dfrac{1}{\Delta}\dfrac{S_L}{\sigma}$
$-\eta_{q\theta}$	0	0	-1

[a]Definitions of variables introduced:

η_{ij} = elasticity of i with respect to j,

S_L = labor share of output; $= (f - kf')/f$,

S_K = capital share of output; $= kf'/f$,

σ = elasticity of substitution; $= d\ln k/d\ln\left(\dfrac{f-kf'}{f'}\right)$,

$\Delta = 1 + \dfrac{1}{\sigma}(\eta_{sr}S_L - \eta_{sy}S_K)$.

small and of uncertain sign. However, Feldstein (1970) has suggested that, because they failed to use the real interest rate, such estimates may have been biased toward zero. After compensating for this and other possible problems, Boskin (1978) has estimated η_{sr} to be much larger than previously anticipated, with a value of about 0.4.

As long as neither first nor second period consumption is an inferior good, η_{sy} is positive. In an economy like the U.S., in which savings is roughly a fixed fraction of income, η_{sy} should be approximately unity. Since S_K, the capital share of output, is about 0.3, $[1 - (S_K/\sigma)\eta_{sy}]$ will be positive unless σ < 0.3, which is implausible.[8]

For the remainder of the analysis we assume that η_{sr} and $[1 - (S_K/\sigma)\eta_{sy}]$ are positive, as seems likely. These assumptions are sufficient, though not necessary, to guarantee that Δ will also be positive.

4.1. Retained earnings and dividends

This is the regime most relevant to current conditions in the U.S., since dividends are paid out, new share issues are small, and the rate of after-tax corporate profits exceeds the growth rate.[9] Total differentiation of (12) for q $= q_D$ and $\delta = 0$ yields the results in the last column of table 2.

Of particular interest are the differences in impact of the three taxes on k and r. The effects of an increase in the corporate tax rate, τ, correspond most closely to those found in earlier work.[10] As long as savings is interest elastic, the lower rate of return induced by the tax leads to a lower steady-state capital stock. This raises the marginal product of capital, so that the net rate of return, r, falls by less than the full tax increase. The fraction of the tax increase which is shifted in this way depends negatively on the degree to which labor may be substituted for capital in production, as represented by the elasticity of substitution, σ.

Since q equals q_D in equilibrium, an increase in τ has no effect on q. Because q_D is determined by θ and c, an increase in either of these tax rates will have a more complicated effect than τ on k and r, since q must also change. (It is easily verified that a simultaneous change in θ and c which leaves q_D unchanged is identical in effect to an increase in τ.) For a given value of q, an increase in θ makes dividends less attractive than retentions, and would lead to greater capital accumulation. For equilibrium to be re-established, q must fall to the new, lower value of q_D, at which firms would once again be willing to distribute dividends. On the other hand, an increase in c would encourage payout of all profits unless q rose. While we are not attempting to model the transition from one steady state to another, one's intuition might suggest that an increase in θ would depress capital accumu-

---

[8]Nerlove (1967) presents an excellent survey of attempts at estimating σ. Time series estimates for aggregate U.S. production generally fall between 0.5 and 0.7. However, cross-section estimates of σ for two-digit SIC industries tend to be much higher than the corresponding time series estimates, suggesting that the aggregate estimates may be too low.

[9]The maximum value of τ in the U.S. is presently 0.46 Feldstein and Summers (1977) have estimated the marginal product of corporate capital to be about 11%. The economy's trend growth rate, taking account of technical change, is lower than the implied value of $f'(1-\tau)$, 5.94%.

[10]See Feldstein (1974), for example.

lation less than an equivalent increase in c, because of these different effects on q_D. In fact, an increase in θ actually leads to an *increase* in the capital–labor ratio, while k is depressed (and f' increased) so much by an increase in c that, for $\eta_{sy} = 1$, r increases when $\sigma < 1$.

The results for this regime indicate that, once equity policy and valuation are accounted for, the effects of an increase in capital income taxation depend on the type of tax change. While a corporate tax increase depresses both the capital–labor ratio and the rate of return, increasing the rate of personal taxation, θ, increases k, while an increase in c, the capital gains tax rate, may depress k so much that r increases.

4.2. Retained earnings and new shares

This regime, which occurs if $f'(1-\tau) < n$, is simpler to describe than the one above, since q is fixed at unity. An increase in τ has the same impact as before. Because q is not a function of c, and since all earnings are retained and thus taxed at the capital gains rate, an increase in c is equivalent to an increase in τ. Similarly, since there are no dividends at the margin, a change in θ, the rate of dividend taxation, has no effect at all.

4.3. Retained earnings only

The intermediate case between those already discussed is that in which q is between q_D and one, so that all earnings are retained, but no new shares are issued. Because dividends are not paid, θ once again has no effect on the equilibrium values of k and r. Since q is endogenous, the results of changing τ or c are unlike those found in either of the above regimes.

The key to the results lies in the fact that $f'(1-\tau) = n$. Thus, an increase in c can have no effect on the equilibrium value of k, so that it will be fully reflected by a drop in r. Since this leads to less saving, q must drop to maintain equality between the capital supplied and demanded in equilibrium. On the other hand, an increase in τ can have no effect on $f'(1-\tau)$, and hence r, so that f' must increase, and k decline, accompanied by an increase in q. Thus, an increase in c is fully reflected in the net rate of return, while an increase in τ is, eventually, completely shifted.

4.4. An example

One case in which there is a unique equilibrium for each set of tax rates, and which may be illustrated diagrammatically, is that in which both production and utility may be represented by Cobb–Douglas functions. The production function is written

$$x = f(k) = ak^\beta, \qquad 0 < \beta < 1. \tag{13}$$

The utility function is

$$U = c_1^\alpha c_2^{(1-\alpha)}, \qquad 0 < \alpha < 1. \tag{14}$$

Utility maximization leads to the savings function

$$s = (1-\alpha)y. \tag{15}$$

Combining (12.1) and (12.3), and using (13) and (15), we obtain

$$q = mf'(k), \tag{16}$$

where m is a constant, not dependent on tax rates. This condition relates q to k, and must hold regardless of regime. It is represented by the line labelled $q(k)$ in fig. 1. It follows immediately that the equilibrium value of k must lie between the values labeled k_1 and k_2, since q is between q_D and one. To solve for equilibrium, we rewrite eq. (12.4) as

$$(n-\delta)/(1-\gamma) = f'(k)(1-\tau), \tag{17}$$

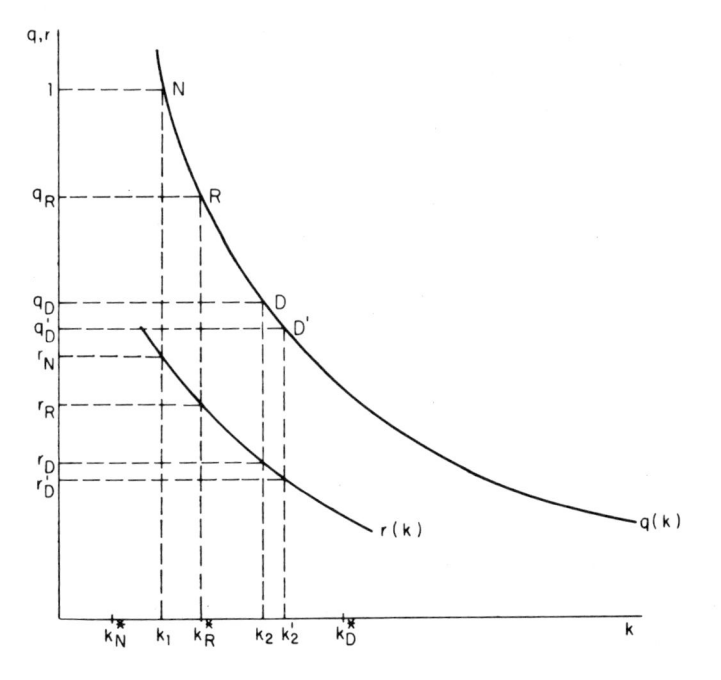

Fig. 1

and let k^* be the value of k obtained by solving (17) for $\delta = \gamma = 0$. Since f'' < 0, if $k < k^*$ then $\gamma > 0$. Similarly, if $k > k^*$, $\delta > 0$. The actual value of k in equilibrium depends on the relation of k^* to k_1 and k_2. Since k must be greater than or equal to k_1, if $k^* < k_1$, then $k^* < k$ and $\delta > 0$. But then we know that $q = 1$, and hence k must equal k_1. Similarly, if k^* exceeds k_2, then $k^* > k$ and $\gamma > 0$, so that $q = q_D$ and $k = k_2$. Finally, if k^* lies between k_1 and k_2, the only possible regime is that with $\delta = \gamma = 0$, so that $k = k^*$ and $q = q(k^*)$. These three possibilities are represented in the diagram by the values k_N^*, k_D^*, and k_R^*, respectively, with corresponding points on $q(k)$ labeled N, D, and R. Equilibrium values of r may be read from the $r(k)$ curve, which represents eq. (12.2).

The effects of tax changes may easily be seen using this diagram. For example, an increase in θ lowers q_D to q_D', which shifts k_2 to k_2'. This has no effect unless there are dividends being paid, in which case k increases to k_2' and r drops to r_D'. A decrease in c would also lower q_D, but would cause an upward shift in the $r(k)$ curve, leading to increases in r_N and r_R and, in this special Cobb–Douglas case, keeping r_D constant. A decrease in τ would also raise $r(k)$, would have no effect on q_D, but would raise k^* [see (17)]. This would increase k and lower q for the intermediate regime, raising the rate of return under each of the other regimes.

5. Conclusions

We have, in this paper, used a simple dynamic model to study the effects of taxes on corporate equity policy. Among our findings are the following.

(1) Capital owned by corporations may well be undervalued, even in the long run.

(2) As a result of such undervaluation, firms may find it in the best interest of their stockholders to distribute dividends.

(3) Firms will finance investment with the sale of new shares only if share price exceeds reproduction cost; on the other hand, retained earnings will be reinvested as long as share price exceeds a value strictly less than reproduction cost.

(4) While tax increases are likely to depress the return to personal saving, an increase in the tax on distributions may lead to an increase in the economy's capital intensity by encouraging the reinvestment of corporate profits.

Much work remains to be done on this subject. A more realistic study of the present problem would incorporate alternative assets, such as bonds and non-corporate capital. Another extension would take into account the progressivity of the actual structure, and the existence of investors with different marginal tax rates.[11]

[11] I have explored some of these issues in later work. See Auerbach (1979).

As stated in the opening section, there are effects other than those considered in this essay which determine corporate equity policy, particularly dividend behavior. Nevertheless, we believe our results to be an important contribution to the understanding of this difficult question.

Appendix

We demonstrate here that, in our model, it will never be advantageous for firms to invest in liquidity rather than capital.

Since the market values capital at q, shareholders will gain from a firm investment in liquid stocks only if the valuation of such stocks is greater per unit than q. Let this value be denoted q_L. Now consider the return an investor can get on that part of a share which represents liquid stocks. If the liquidity is taken as a dividend, the investor receives one dollar for every q_L dollars invested, which is taxed at rate θ, yielding a return of

$$r_D^L = \frac{1-\theta}{q_L} - 1. \tag{A1}$$

Since $q_L \geq q \geq (1-\theta)/(1-c) > (1-\theta)$, r_D^L is negative.

If the stocks are invested in capital, the capital will have less value, since $q < q_L$. Thus, the return upon sale will be negative. Finally, if the stocks are held for one period, they maintain their value, yielding a return of zero. Since $r_R = f'(1-\tau)(1-c) > 0$, firms will never hold any liquid stocks.

References

Auerbach, A.J., 1979, Wealth maximization and the cost of capital, Quarterly Journal of Economics 93, forthcoming.

Boskin, M.J., 1978, Taxation, saving and the rate of interest, Journal of Political Economy 86, S3–S27.

Diamond, P.A., 1965, Debt in a neoclassical growth model, American Economic Review 55, 1126–1150.

Diamond, P.A., 1970, Incidence of an interest income tax, Journal of Economic Theory 2, 211–224.

Farrar, D.F. and L.L. Selwyn, 1967, Taxes, corporate financial policy and return to investors, National Tax Journal 20, 444–454.

Feldstein, M.S., 1970, Inflation, specification bias and the impact on interest rates, Journal of Political Economy 78, 1325–1339.

Feldstein, M.S., 1974, Incidence of a capital income tax in a growing economy with variable savings rates, Review of Economic Studies 41, 505–513.

Feldstein, M.S. and L. Summers, 1977, Is the rate of profit falling?, Brookings Papers on Economic Activity, 211–228.

Feldstein, M.S., J. Green and E. Sheshinski, 1979, Corporate financial policy and taxation in a growing economy, Quarterly Journal of Economics 93, forthcoming.

Flemming, J.S., 1976, A reappraisal of the corporation income tax, Journal of Public Economics 6, 163–169.

Gordon, M.J., 1962, The investment financing and valuation of the corporation (Irwin, Homewood, Ill.).

King, M.A., 1974, Taxation and the cost of capital, Review of Economic Studies 41, 21–35.
Modigliani, F. and M.H. Miller, 1958, The cost of capital, corporation finance and the theory of investment, American Economic Review 48, 261–297.
Nerlove, M., 1967, Recent empirical studies of the CES and related production functions, in: M. Brown, ed., The theory and empirical analysis of production (NBER, New York).
Pye, G., 1972, Preferential tax treatment of capital gains, optimal dividend policy, and capital budgeting, Quarterly Journal of Economics 86, 226–242.
Stapleton, R.C., 1972, Taxes, the cost of capital and the theory of investment, Economic Journal 82, 1273–1292.
Stiglitz, J.E., 1973, Taxation, corporate financial policy, and the cost of capital, Journal of Public Economics 2, 1–34.
Stiglitz, J.E., 1976, The corporation tax, Journal of Public Economics 5, 303–311.
Tobin, J., 1969, A general equilibrium approach to monetary theory, Journal of Money, Credit and Banking 1, 15–29.

5

Wealth Maximization and the Cost of Capital

I. INTRODUCTION

In a simple world of certainty, with perfect capital markets, no taxes on capital income, and all investment financed through direct ownership, a utility-maximizing investor would strive to maximize the present value of his investment. This wealth maximization would be achieved by the acceptance of all investment projects having a positive present value when discounted at the individual's personal rate of time preference.

Once the possibility of corporate finance is introduced, complications arise concerning the optimal choice of financing method and the appropriate discount rate to use in present value calculations. In the absence of taxation certain principles are generally accepted. First, it is irrelevant whether equity-source investment funds come from retained earnings or the sale of new shares. Second, firms should use a composite "cost of capital" in their discounting decisions, a weighted average of the interest rate on debt and the rate of time preference of stockholders. Finally, if the cost of capital varies with the degree of debt finance, or "leverage," [1] firms should choose the debt-equity ratio for which it is minimized. While many authors have arrived at these results starting from the objective of wealth maximization, the exact relationship remains somewhat unclear. In addition, there has been considerable debate over the impact of corporate and personal income taxes on firm policy.[2]

In this paper we explore the issue of wealth maximization and the implied behavior of the firm, paying particular attention to the results discussed above and how they are affected by the existence

The author would like to thank Martin Feldstein and Jerry Green for many stimulating discussions relating to this topic.

1. Modigliani and Miller [1958] have argued that, in the absence of taxation, it cannot.

2. See Farrar and Selwyn [1967], Pye [1972], Stapleton [1972], Stiglitz [1973, 1976], King [1974], Miller [1977], Auerbach [1979], and Bradford [1978].

of capital income taxes. Our results indicate that a tax structure similar to that in existence in the United States influences the cost of capital in a very different way than has been assumed previously and that the relative advantages of debt over equity as a method of finance, and capital gains over dividends as a vehicle for personal realization of corporate profits, may have been greatly overstated. These findings may help to explain certain aspects of corporate financial behavior that have seemed puzzling.

II. The Model

We consider the behavior of competitive firms in a discrete-time, infinite-horizon model. These firms finance their investment projects through sales of common stock, retention of earnings, and sales of debt, which, for the sake of simplicity, we take to have a term of one period. At the beginning of each period, firms distribute dividends to pre-existing shareholders, pay interest, and repay principal on debt outstanding in the previous period, and sell new shares, ex dividend. Corporate profits are taxed at rate τ, but interest payments may be deducted from taxable profits. Dividends are taxed at rate θ at the personal level. We assume that capital gains are taxed upon accrual at a rate $c < \theta$. We thus abstract from the issue of tax deferment that arises when, as in the United States, capital gains are taxed upon realization, and concentrate on the favorable rate at which capital gains, relative to dividends, are taxed. All stockholders face the same personal tax rates, θ and c.

The one-period discount rate of equity owners during period t is ρ_t,[3] while the interest rate is i_t. The ex dividend value of pre-existing shares at the beginning of period t is denoted V_t^0. The value of new equity sold is V_t^N. Thus, the ex dividend value of the firm's equity at the beginning of period t is

$$(1) \qquad V_t = V_t^0 + V_t^N.$$

The degree to which equity is "diluted" by new equity sales may be represented by the fraction,

$$(2) \qquad \delta_t = V_t^N / V_t.$$

Debt outstanding in period t is B_t, and the firm's "leverage" is defined by the term,

$$(3) \qquad b_t = B_t / (B_t + V_t).$$

3. Note that ρ is the rate at which stockholders discount *nominal* flows from equity. If inflation is present, at rate π, the real discount rate is $\rho - \pi$.

If we let x_t represent the cash flow of the firm at the beginning of period t, net of corporate tax, but before account is taken of net sales of debt and equity, interest payments, and the tax savings on such payments, then dividends paid at the beginning of period $t + 1$ (i.e., the end of period t) on shares held during period t are

(4) $$D_t = x_{t+1} + B_{t+1} + V_{t+1}^N - [1 + i_t(1 - \tau)]B_t.$$

By the very definition of dividends, D must always be nonnegative.

III. The Problem

We assume that firms seek to maximize the wealth of existing shareholders. This is accomplished by choosing, at the beginning of period t, an investment policy, represented by the vector $\tilde{\mathbf{x}} = (x_t, x_{t+1}, \ldots)$, a debt policy, $\mathbf{B} = (B_t, B_{t+1}, \ldots)$, and an equity policy, $\mathbf{V}^N = (V_t^N, V_{t+1}^N, \ldots)$,[4] which, among feasible choices, maximize the value of shares owned as of the beginning of period t, including the concurrent after-tax distribution.

Before proceeding any further, we must derive an expression for the valuation of equity. We assume that shares are equal in value to the present discounted value of the distributions their owners receive. At the end of period t, the total dividends paid to all stockholders are D_t. However, if there are personal taxes, the net distribution is smaller. The personal tax liability at the end of period t is the tax on dividends θD_t, plus that on accrued capital gains on existing stock, $c(V_{t+1}^0 - V_t)$. Thus, the net distribution received by all shareholders at the end of period t is

(5) $$E_t = (1 - \theta)D_t - c(V_{t+1}^0 - V_t).$$

If new equity is issued between period t and a subsequent period s, not all of the distribution E_s will go to shares held as of period t. A fraction will go to the shares arising from the new issues. The fraction of shares held during period s that were in existence before the start of period t is, from (2),

(6) $$\mu_t^s = (1 - \delta_t)(1 - \delta_{t+1}) \ldots (1 - \delta_s).$$

Thus, the distribution at time $s \geq t$ to shares owned as of the beginning of period t is $\mu_t^s E_s$, and the value of such equity is

(7) $$V_t^0 = \sum_{s=t}^{\infty} \left[\prod_{z=t}^{s} (1 + \rho_z)^{-1} \right] \mu_t^s E_s.$$

4. The choice of $\tilde{\mathbf{x}}$, $\tilde{\mathbf{B}}$, and $\tilde{\mathbf{V}}^N$ determines the dividend policy $\tilde{\mathbf{D}} = (D_{t-1}, D_t, \ldots)$.

Using (1) and (2), and applying (7) for successive values of t, we obtain

(8) $$\rho_t V_t = E_t + (V_{t+1}^0 - V_t).$$

Equation (8) states that, for all t, the one-period holding yield on equity, which includes the net distribution and capital gain, must equal the rate of time preference associated with equity holding ρ_t.

The wealth of existing stockholders that the firm seeks to maximize is

(9) $$W_t^0 = V_t^0 + E_{t-1}.$$

Using (1), (4), and (5), we may rewrite this expression as

(10) $$\begin{aligned} W_t^0 = & (1 - c)V_t + (1 - \theta) \\ & \times \{B_t - [1 + i_{t-1}(1 - \tau)]B_{t-1} + x_t\} \\ & - (\theta - c)V_t^N + {}_cV_{t-1}. \end{aligned}$$

Since i_{t-1}, V_{t-1}, and B_{t-1} are predetermined at the beginning of period t, W_t^0 is maximized if and only if the firm maximizes

(11) $$W_t^* = (1 - c)V_t + (1 - \theta)B_t + (1 - \theta)x_t - (\theta - c)V_t^N.$$

We are now ready to examine the characteristics of wealth-maximizing behavior. Because of the complexity of the general problem, we attack first the simpler case in which $\theta = c = 0$.

IV. WEALTH MAXIMIZATION: NO PERSONAL TAXES

In this situation the firm's objective function (11) reduces to

(12) $$W_t^* = V_t + B_t + x_t.$$

Firms desire to maximize the sum of their securities' market value and current cash flow. This is a standard result.

To simplify the exposition in this and succeeding sections, we introduce the term,

(13) $$F_t = D_t - V_{t+1}^N,$$

which is the dividend payable at the end of period t, before account is taken of the sale of new equity.

Using (1), (5), (8), and (13), we obtain for the case with no personal taxes

(14) $$V_t = (1 + \rho_t)^{-1}(V_{t+1} + F_t).$$

Solving for V_t, we obtain[5]

$$(15) \qquad V_t = \sum_{s=t}^{\infty} \left[\prod_{z=t}^{s} (1 + \rho_z)^{-1} \right] F_s.$$

Thus, as first argued by Miller and Modigliani [1961], the particular source of equity funds used to finance investment has no impact on the firm valuation. Once $\mathbf{x}$ and $\mathbf{B}$ are determined, so is V_t, since F is, by definition, independent of V^N. Because of this result, we may ignore the question of share sales and repurchases when considering the question of wealth maximization in the absence of personal taxes.

Using expressions (1) and (13) to substitute into (14), and then rearranging terms, we obtain an expression for shareholder wealth:

$$(16) \qquad W_t^* = x_t + (1 + r_t)^{-1} W_{t+1}^*,$$

where we define the term,

$$(17) \qquad r_t = b_t i_t (1 - \tau) + (1 - b_t) \rho_t,$$

to be the "cost of capital," an average of the returns the firm must earn on equity holdings and debt, weighted by their respective portions in the firm financial structure. Because of the deductibility of interest payments, the net cost of debt is $i_t(1 - \tau)$, rather than the gross interest rate.

Solving (16) for W_t^*, we obtain[6]

$$(18) \qquad W_t^* = x_t + \sum_{s=t+1}^{\infty} \left[\prod_{z=t}^{s-1} (1 + r_z)^{-1} \right] x_s.$$

Shareholder wealth may be expressed as the present value of the stream of after-tax corporate cash flows, where the financial policy determines the appropriate discount rate.

It is clear that the cost of capital, defined above, determines the cutoff point for investment projects. Given the choice of financial policy and, hence, the value of $\mathbf{r} = (r_t, r_{t+1}, \ldots)$, the firm will increase W_t^* by accepting those projects having positive present value when the cost of capital in each period is used as the discount rate.

Up until this point we have said very little about the determi-

5. This result is dependent on the assumption that the term $\prod_{z=t}^{T} (1 + \rho_z)^{-1} V_T$ approaches zero as T approaches infinity; that is, the firm's value grows at a rate less than ρ. This restriction is necessary to rule out "chain letters" in which F is continually less than or equal to zero and dividends on existing shares are supported solely by the sale of new shares. A similar assumption will be made concerning the value of W_t^* in equation (18) to rule out the continual sale of ever larger amounts of new debt to support payments to existing holders of debt and equity.

6. See note 5.

nation of ρ and i, or about the place of risk in our model. A completely adequate treatment of risk is beyond the scope of this paper. It is even questionable whether firms should always seek to maximize share-holder wealth when there is uncertainty as to the particular state of nature that will occur in each period. One fairly simple, albeit im-perfect, approach is to assume that the market evaluation of a firm's "riskiness" increases with the degree of leverage, and that the required rates of return ρ and i must increase;[7] that is,

$$(19) \qquad \rho_t = \rho(b_t), \quad i_t = i(b_t), \quad \rho', i' > 0.$$

If we assume that ρ_t and i_t are determined in this way, it follows from (17) and (18) that, for any given stream $\mathbf{x}$, the firm maximizes W_t^* by choosing b_s for each period $s \geq t$ to minimize the cost of capital. Thus, the overall wealth maximization, in this case, may be viewed as a two-stage procedure in which firms first determine the financial policy that minimizes the cost of capital faced in each period, and then use this cost of capital as the discount rate in determining the optimal investment strategy.

V. Wealth Maximization with Personal Taxes

A more interesting, and more difficult, problem arises once we remove the assumption that $\theta = c = 0$. Many of the familiar results of the previous case must be altered to take account of the existence of personal taxes.

The first difference, seen in the definition of W^* (in equation (11)) is that the firm should not strive to maximize the sum of current cash flow and the market value of its securities, unless $\theta = c$. This condition is, in our model, equivalent to the integration of corporate and personal income taxes, since all corporate source income, whether retained or distributed, would be taxed at the same rate; $\tau' = \tau + \theta = \tau + c$.

Following the same procedure used to obtain equation (15), we get, after various substitutions,

$$(20) \quad V_t = \sum_{s=t}^{\infty} \left[\sum_{z=t}^{s} \left(1 + \frac{\rho_z}{1-c} \right)^{-1} \right] \left[\left(\frac{1-\theta}{1-c} \right) F_s - \left(\frac{\theta-c}{1-c} \right) V_{s+1}^N \right].$$

Comparing (20) to (15), we note that, unless $\theta = c$, taxes enter in a complex way into the valuation formula. However, there is one ex-tremely important observation that can be made. For any given values

---

7. See Feldstein, Green, and Sheshinski [1979] for a recent example of this ap-proach.

of $\mathbf{x}$ and $\mathbf{B}$, and hence $\mathbf{F}$, a decrease in the net issue of new equity, V_s^N, at any time $s > t$, increases V_t and hence W_t^*, since $\theta > c$. Thus, it will never be optimal to issue new shares and pay dividends at the same time, since V_t may be increased by an equal decrease in D_{s-1} and V_s^N.

The same logic would compel firms to continue decreasing V^N below zero, repurchasing equity, as long as dividends were positive, if such behavior were not otherwise hindered. This dominance of share repurchases over dividends as a method of distribution has been recognized in the past by many authors.[8] However, share repurchases have never constituted an important part of firm distributions. Part of the answer probably lies in Section 302 of the Internal Revenue Code, which prohibits firms from repurchasing shares in lieu of distributing dividends.

Recent U. S. data confirm that new share issues have constituted only a small portion of new equity finance, and that repurchases have been a very unimportant method of distribution, compared to dividends. For example, in 1976, net issues of debt by U. S. nonfinancial corporations amounted to $47.8 billion, retained earnings were $44.3 billion, and dividends were $32.2 billion. Net issues of equity were only $10.5 billion,[9] and share repurchases were, in turn, only a small percentage of this number.[10]

Given the above discussion, we shall henceforth assume that firms neither issue new shares nor repurchase existing ones. While not greatly abstracting from reality, this restriction constitutes a very helpful simplification. Assuming that $V_t^N \equiv 0$, we see that (20) becomes

$$(21) \qquad V_t = \sum_{s=t}^{\infty} \left[\prod_{z=t}^{s} \left(1 + \frac{\rho_z}{1-c} \right)^{-1} \right] \left(\frac{1-\theta}{1-c} \right) F_s.$$

Following the same procedure used in deriving (18), we obtain

$$(22) \qquad W_t^* = (1 - \theta) \left[x_t + \sum_{s=t+1}^{\infty} \left(\prod_{z=t}^{s-1} (1 + r_z)^{-1} \right) x_s \right],$$

where the cost of capital is

---

8. Among them, Bierman and West [1966], Pye [1972], and King [1974].
9. The preceding figures were obtained from the 1976:IV issue of the *Flow of Funds Accounts* published by the Board of Governors of the Federal Reserve System.
10. The breakdown between new issues and repurchases is not given for nonfinancial corporations. However, the corresponding figures for all corporate business in 1976 are listed in the December 1977 issue of the *Federal Reserve Bulletin*. While gross sales of new equity amounted to $14.1 billion, repurchases were only $3.1 billion.

(23) $\quad r_t = [(1 - c) - (\theta - c)b_t]^{-1}[b_t i_t (1 - \tau)(1 - \theta) + (1 - b_t)\rho_t]$.

As in the case without personal taxes, the firm maximizes wealth, given financial policy, by choosing all projects that have a positive present value when discounted by the cost of capital, and if i and ρ are determined by (19), should choose the degree of leverage that minimizes the cost of capital.

The formula for the cost of capital given in (23) differs from results obtained previously, and there are a number of interesting observations to be made concerning this expression. If the firm is financed solely through debt, then r reduces to the net of tax rate of interest, $i(1 - \tau)$, which the firm must pay on its debt. At the other extreme, an equity-financed firm faces a cost of capital of $\rho/(1 - c)$. There are two rather surprising aspects of this result. First, the cost of capital does not depend on the dividend payout rate. Second, the rate of dividend taxation does not enter at all. Equity gains are effectively taxed at rate c, which may be very small compared to the statutory rate of taxation of dividends. Even for the general case in which there is both debt and equity in the firm, the payout rate does not directly influence the cost of capital.

The next section contains an example that should aid in the understanding of the above results.

VI. FIRM VALUE AND THE COST OF CAPITAL

In this section we consider the particular case of an economy in which there is no inflation, in which i, ρ, b, and hence r, are all constant, and assume that firms produce output using homogeneous, nondepreciating capital and labor, subject to a constant-returns-to-scale technology. These assumptions are made to facilitate the exposition and do not influence the characteristics of the results.

The investment in an additional unit of capital at any given time t will decrease concurrent cash flow by the purchase price, and increase the cash flow in each succeeding period by the marginal product of such capital, less corporate taxes, $f'(1 - \tau)$. Such a project increases W_t^* by $[f'(1 - \tau)/r] - 1$. Perfect competition ensures that firms will invest until the adoption of new projects does not increase wealth; that is, the after-tax marginal product of capital must equal the cost of capital:

(24) $\qquad\qquad f'(1 - \tau) = r$.

Given that firms equate the wage rate with the marginal product of labor, the cash flow available to the firm at the beginning of period

t if no new investment occurs is, by Euler's Theorem, $f'(1 - \tau)K_{t-1}$, where K_{t-1} is the capital on hand during period $t - 1$. The net cash flow at the beginning of period t is therefore this amount less new investment:

(25) $x_t = f'(1 - \tau)K_{t-1} - (K_t - K_{t-1}).$

Using (22), (24), and (25), we obtain

$$(26) \quad W_t^* = (1 - \theta)\left\{x_t + \sum_{s=t-1}^{\infty} (1 + r)^{-(s-t)}[(1 + r)K_{s-1} - K_s]\right\}$$

$$= (1 - \theta)[x_t + K_t].$$

Substituting (26) into (11), we obtain

$$(27) \qquad\qquad V_t = \left(\frac{1 - \theta}{1 - c}\right)[K_t - B_t],$$

which is similar to results obtained by Auerbach [1978] for the case of all equity finance and Bradford [1978] for the case in which $\tau = c = 0$. Since $\theta > c$, the market value of equity is lower than the reproduction cost of its capital stock, less the market value of its debt. In the language of Tobin [1969], "q" is less than unity.

Since this capitalization occurs, the presumed superiority of capital gains over dividends disappears, and the effective tax on equity income is lower than a weighted average of the statutory taxes on dividends and capital gains. For example, imagine an all-equity firm considering taking one dollar out of current dividends for reinvestment. The net loss to stockholders in the current period is $(1 - \theta)$, since their dividend tax liability is also reduced. The capital stock is increased by one unit, and by (27) the stock's market value goes up by $(1 - \theta)/(1 - c)$. Therefore, current capital gains taxes are increased by $c(1 - \theta)/(1 - c)$. If the stockholders then sell off the value of the stock corresponding to the new investment, they receive a capital gain of $(1 - \theta)/(1 - c)$, and the value of their remaining stock is the same as it would have been if the dividend had been paid out. But the total distribution is $(1 - \theta)/(1 - c) - c(1 - \theta)/(1 - c) = (1 - \theta)$, which equals the dividend foregone. Thus, payout policy is irrelevant from the point of view of the stockholders.

Now, suppose that instead of selling off the increase in stock value, individuals hold it forever. Also, suppose that all returns from the new capital in succeeding periods are paid out in dividends. (Since we have just demonstrated the irrelevance of payout policy, this assumption poses no restrictions.) The initial cost is then the lost dividend $(1 - \theta)$, plus the capital gains tax accrued $c(1 - \theta)/(1 - c)$, for

a total of $(1 - \theta)/(1 - c)$. The net distribution in each period is the marginal product of capital, less corporate and dividend taxes, $f'(1 - \tau)(1 - \theta)$. Thus, this marginal asset has zero present value, discounted at ρ, when $f'(1 - \tau) = \rho/(1 - c)$, the all-equity cost of capital derived in the previous section.[11]

VII. FINANCIAL POLICY AND THE COST OF CAPITAL

Thus far, we have had little to say about the choice of financial mix between debt and equity. One important question to ask is whether, in the absence of any notion of risk or bankruptcy, firms will finance with both equity and debt or, as has been suggested by Stiglitz [1973], will finance with only debt at the margin.

If all future streams are certain, then the degree of leverage of a firm has no impact on the values of ρ and i that it faces. Shares in all firms are perfect substitutes, as are bonds, so that firms are price-takers with respect to ρ and i.

Differentiating (23) with respect to b, for i and ρ constant, we obtain (dropping subscripts)

$$(28) \quad \frac{dr}{db} = [(1 - c) - (\theta - c)b]^{-2}(1 - \theta)[i(1 - \tau)(1 - c) - \rho],$$

which is either always positive, always negative, or always zero. Thus, firms will desire all debt if $i(1 - \tau)(1 - c) < \rho$, all equity if $i(1 - \tau)(1 - c) > \rho$, and be indifferent if $i(1 - \tau)(1 - c) = \rho$. The determination of i and ρ depends, in turn, on the characteristics of individual investors. We consider two cases, one in which all investors face the same tax schedule, the second in which they do not. In each case we let ϕ denote the individual tax rate on debt income.

Case 1: One Class of Investors

Without risk, debt and equity should be perfect substitutes, and investors will hold whichever yields a higher net rate of return, holding both only if these returns are equal. For an equilibrium to exist with debt and equity present, both firms and individuals must be indifferent between the alternatives. From our discussion above, the condition for firm indifference is $i(1 - \tau)(1 - c) = \rho$. By construction, individuals receive ρ from holding equity. After paying a personal

11. There is a question as to whether this undervaluation equilibrium is feasible. In another paper we explored this problem in the context of an all-equity, overlapping-generations growth model (Auerbach, 1979) and found that such a regime could occur there only if the after-tax marginal product of capital, $f'(1 - \tau)$, exceeds the population growth rate.

income tax, they receive $i(1 - \phi)$ from holding debt. Thus, individuals will be indifferent if and only if $i(1 - \phi) = \rho$. Combining these two conditions, we have the result that debt and equity will exist together in equilibrium if and only if $(1 - \tau)(1 - c) = (1 - \phi)$.

Now assume that we are initially in a position in which both debt and equity are held, so that $i(1 - \phi) = \rho$, and suppose that $(1 - \tau)(1 - c) > (1 - \phi)$. Then $i(1 - \tau)(1 - c) > \rho$, and firms will shift entirely to equity. Similarly, if $(1 - \tau)(1 - c) < (1 - \phi)$, they will shift entirely to debt. Thus, the equilibrium will be characterized by all equity, all debt, or both according to whether $(1 - \tau)(1 - c)$ is greater than, less than, or equal to $(1 - \phi)$.[12]

It is interesting that the tax on dividends θ does not enter directly into the process at all.[13] Since the question of which method of finance will be used depends on c, it would be helpful to relate this hypothetical tax on accrued capital gains to the currently existing tax on realized gains. Bailey [1969] has shown that the effective tax rate on accrued capital gains approximately equals the statutory rate on realizations, which cannot exceed 0.5θ, times the ratio of realizations to accruals, which he estimated to be 0.2 for the long run in the United States. If we let $c = 0.1\theta$ and assume that $\theta = \phi$, then the equilibrium will be characterized by all equity, all debt, or both according to whether θ is greater than, less than, or equal to $\bar{\theta}$, where

(29) $$\bar{\theta} = \tau/(0.9 + 0.1\tau).$$

If we take τ to be the U. S. statutory rate 0.46, then $\bar{\theta} = 0.486$. That is, an all-debt equilibrium will occur only if $\bar{\theta} < 0.506$. In comparison, the maximum statutory rate on personal capital income in the United States is presently 0.7.

In the model just presented, an equilibrium will have all equity or all debt according to whether or not "the" tax rate on personal income exceeds $\bar{\theta}$. In reality, however, the marginal tax rates faced by individuals vary greatly.

Case 2: Two Classes of Investors

Suppose that there are investors of two types, differing only by their marginal tax rates. Let (θ_1, ϕ_1, c_1) be the rates faced by class 1, and let (θ_2, ϕ_2, c_2) be those faced by class 2. For simplicity, we again assume that $\theta_1 = \phi_1$ and $\theta_2 = \phi_2$. Our objective is to derive the conditions under which debt and equity coexist in equilibrium, with one

12. A similar result has been derived by King [1974].
13. Bradford [1978] has demonstrated this point for the case in which $\tau = c = \phi = 0$.

class holding equity and the other debt. For this to occur, firms must be indifferent between debt and equity, equity-holders must prefer equity, and debt-holders must prefer debt. Without any loss of generality, we take class 1 to be the equity-holders.

In equilibrium the rate of return received by equity investors must equal their rate of time preference. Combining (5) and (8), we obtain

$$(30) \qquad \rho^1 = (1 - \theta_1)\frac{D}{V} + (1 - c_1)\frac{\Delta V}{V},$$

where ρ^1 is the rate of time preference of class 1 members and ΔV is the capital gain they receive. Similarly, the net return to holders of debt must equal their rate of time preference:

$$(31) \qquad \rho^2 = (1 - \phi_2)i.$$

The potential return to equity holders from holding debt is

$$(32) \qquad \rho^{1*} = (1 - \phi_1)i,$$

and the potential return to debt holders from holding equity is

$$(33) \qquad \rho^{2*} = (1 - \theta_2)\frac{D}{V} + (1 - c_2)\frac{\Delta V}{V}.$$

The conditions for an equilibrium with debt and equity are

$$(34.1) \qquad \rho^1 \geq \rho^{1*}$$

$$(34.2) \qquad \rho^2 \geq \rho^{2*}$$

$$(34.3) \qquad i(1 - \tau)(1 - c_1) = \rho^1;$$

that is, debt-holders prefer debt, equity-holders prefer equity, and firms are indifferent between debt and equity. Combining (30)–(34) (and substituting θ_1 for ϕ_1 and θ_2 for ϕ_2), we obtain

$$(35) \qquad \left(\frac{1 - \theta_1}{1 - c_1}\right)\left[\frac{((1 - c_1)/(1 - \theta_1))(1 - \alpha) + \alpha}{((1 - c_2)/(1 - \theta_2))(1 - \alpha) + \alpha}\right] \geq (1 - \tau) \geq \left(\frac{1 - \theta_1}{1 - c_1}\right),$$

where α is the fraction of gross equity gains received through dividends:

$$(36) \qquad \alpha = \frac{D}{\Delta V + D}.$$

It is clear that (35) can hold only if $(1 - c_1)/(1 - \theta_1) \geq (1 - c_2)/(1 - \theta_2)$. (Since we may rearrange indices, this is always possible.) What this tells us is that if equity and debt coexist in equilibrium, equity

must be held by those who receive a relatively greater tax advantage in the statutory treatment of capital gains. This result is similar to that of the simple Ricardian trade model which dictates that countries will specialize in the production of the good for which they have a *comparative* advantage.

If $(1 - c_1)/(1 - \theta_1) = (1 - c_2)/(1 - \theta_2)$, then condition (35) will be met if and only if $(1 - \tau) = (1 - \theta_1)/(1 - c_1) = (1 - \theta_2)/(1 - c_2)$, in which case both classes will be indifferent between debt and equity. Thus, the two-class example collapses to the one-class example, and no segmentation will occur. Suppose, at the other extreme, that class 2 consists of tax-exempt investors, such as nonprofit institutions. Then (35) becomes

$$(37) \qquad (1 - \alpha) + \alpha \left(\frac{1 - \theta_1}{1 - c_1}\right) \geq (1 - \tau) \geq \left(\frac{1 - \theta_1}{1 - c_1}\right).$$

Unless α is near unity,[14] the first inequality in (37) will be satisfied, and the condition reduces to that necessary for the existence of equity in a one-class economy. Thus, in a two-class world, with one class tax-exempt, and the other facing a marginal tax rate on regular capital income between 0.51 and 0.70, debt and equity would coexist, with the former group holding debt and the latter holding equity.

VIII. Conclusion

This paper has reviewed the investment and financial behavior of corporations seeking to maximize the wealth of their shareholders. We have focused on the impact of personal income and capital gains taxes, finding that, in the presence of differential taxation of dividends and capital gains, wealth maximization does not imply maximization of firm market value and the source of equity financing is not irrelevant.

The appropriate cost of capital in the presence of personal taxes does not depend directly on either the dividend payout rate or the tax on dividends. Equity shares have a market value lower than the difference between the reproduction cost of a firm's assets and the market value of its debt obligations. Because of this capitalization, it need not be true that an economy without risk or uncertainty would have no equity financing.

---

14. For $c = 0.1 \cdot \theta$, $\theta \leq 0.70$, and $\tau = 0.46$, the first inequality in (37) must hold unless $\alpha \geq 0.68$.

References

Auerbach, A. J., "Share Valuation and Corporate Equity Policy," *Journal of Public Economics,* 1979.

Bailey, M. J., "Capital Gains and Income Taxation," in A. C. Harberger and M. J. Bailey, eds., *The Taxation of Income from Capital* (Washington, D.C.: Brookings Institution, 1969).

Bierman, H., and R. West, "The Acquisition of Common Stock by the Corporate Issuer," *Journal of Finance,* XXI (Dec. 1966), 687–96.

Bradford, D., "The Incidence and Allocation Effects of a Tax on Corporate Distributions," mimeographed, 1978.

Farrar, D. F., and L. L. Selwyn, "Taxes, Corporate Financial Policy, and Return to Investors," *National Tax Journal,* XX (Dec. 1967), 444–54.

Feldstein, M. S., J. Green, and E. Sheshinski, "Corporate Financial Policy and Taxation in a Growing Economy," this *Journal,* XCIII (Aug. 1979), 411–32.

King, M. A., "Taxation and the Cost of Capital," *Review of Economic Studies,* XLI (Jan. 1974), 21–35.

Miller, M. H., "Debt and Taxes," *Journal of Finance,* XXXII (May 1977), 261–75.

——, and F. Modigliani, "Dividend Policy, Growth, and the Valuation of Shares," *Journal of Business,* XXXIV (Oct. 1961), 411–33.

Modigliani, F., and M. H. Miller, "The Cost of Capital, Corporation Finance, and the Theory of Investment," *American Economic Review,* XLVIII (June 1958), 261–97.

Pye, G., "Preferential Tax Treatment of Capital Gains, Optimal Dividend Policy, and Capital Budgeting," this *Journal,* LXXXVI (May 1972), 226–42.

Stapleton, R. C., "Taxes, the Cost of Capital, and the Theory of Investment," *Economic Journal,* LXXXII (Dec. 1972), 1273–92.

Stiglitz, J. E., "Taxation, Corporate Financial Policy, and the Cost of Capital," *Journal of Public Economics,* II (Feb. 1973), 1–34.

——, "The Corporation Tax," *Journal of Public Economics,* V (April 1976), 303–11.

Tobin, J., "A General Equilibrium Approach to Monetary Theory," *Journal of Money, Credit and Banking,* I (Feb. 1969), 15–29.

U.S. Federal Reserve System, Board of Governors, *Flow of Funds Accounts.*

——, *Federal Reserve Bulletin,* LXIII (Dec. 1977).

PART III
INFLATION AND THE FIRM

The prolonged period of substantial inflation in the 1970s posed a new dilemma for the U.S. tax system. Among the many channels through which inflation might affect investment and financial behavior by firms is the way it changes the measurement of income under the income tax. As discussed earlier, the income an owner receives from an asset equals the cash flow it generates plus any change in the asset's value. For financial assets, the latter item is called the capital gain (or loss). For physical or real assets, it is called depreciation, since it is normally assumed that the value will decline. Pure income taxation would be based on this measure.

Without inflation, neither the corporate nor the personal "income" tax in the United States actually has income as its base. In the former case, depreciation allowances do not equal actual economic depreciation, and some investment purchases receive the investment tax credit. In the latter case, capital gains are taxed not at full income tax rates on accrual, but rather at preferential rates on realization. Certainly, the combined base of corporate and personal taxes in no way resembles the actual income being generated by the real assets that individuals own through corporations. This means that the effective corporate and personal tax rates differ from their statutory counterparts, and the overall effective tax rate depends on each separate effective tax rate in a complicated manner. Though difficult to compute, this last number is probably most relevant in gauging the impact of the tax system on the incentive for corporations to invest.

Inflation changes all of these effective tax rates. This does not occur because of the initial deviations from income as a tax base, but because nominal rather than real magnitudes are used in computing capital gains on financial assets and depreciation on physical assets. Under uniform inflation, all assets rise in nominal value by a rate equal to their real rise (or decline) plus the inflation rate. Thus, each asset is subject to an "inflation tax" equal to the tax rate that its gains are normally subject to multiplied by the inflation rate. This affects the corporation's capital investment decision directly by raising the tax on physical and on financial assets. Since the typical corporation holds negative quantities of financial assets (i.e., is a net borrower), it gains from the increased tax on financial assets: its deductions in-

crease. Thus, at the corporate level, there are a gain and a loss, the magnitudes of which may be similar.

Individuals holding the corporation's securities are affected, too. But since net holdings of debt and equity by the household sector are both positive, the additional tax due to inflation is unambiguously positive. The overall effect of inflation on the effective tax rate of corporate and personal income taxes combined is analyzed in "Inflation and the Tax Treatment of Firm Behavior." Also studied are the effects on the relative taxation of equity-financed and debt-financed capital, the decision concerning whether to keep or replace plant and equipment, and the choice of asset life.

The durability decision is an important issue, studied in greater detail in "Inflation and the Choice of Asset Life." Some common wisdom suggests that the "inflation tax" on depreciation allowances is heaviest for long-lived assets, since these assets receive their allowances in the more distant future. But this assumption is misleading. While such allowances are reduced in value by a greater percentage for longer-lived assets, their total value is smaller to begin with, and the latter characteristic dominates the former. However, this does not necessarily mean that inflation will cause more investment in long-lived versus short-lived assets, because other effects are at work in the opposite direction when inflation increases, including the overall increase in the effective tax rate on assets.

Proper methods of dealing with inflation have been the subject of a great many papers, but national economic policy has gone its own way. The standard and straightforward approach to insulating the effective tax rates on investment from inflation is indexing: stating the capital gain or depreciation component of income in real terms. Explicit schemes for indexing the capital gains tax, the tax on interest income, and depreciation schedules have all been proposed (see, for example, Auerbach and Jorgenson, "Inflation-Proof Depreciation of Assets," Harvard Business Review 58 [September-October 1980], 113-118), but in each case Congress has reacted to inflation by reducing the effective tax rate indirectly. This was accomplished by reducing to forty percent the taxed fraction of long-term capital gains in 1978, and most recently by enacting the Accelerated Cost Recovery System for depreciation allowances as part of the Economic Recovery Tax Act of 1981. While perhaps easier to adopt than direct indexing, such plans do not eradicate the effect of changes in the inflation rate on effective tax rates. This is because although tax rates have been lowered, they are still applied to nominal income bases.

6

Inflation and the Tax Treatment of Firm Behavior

In the past decade, economists have begun to realize that inflation, even when fully anticipated, constitutes a great deal more than a tax on money balances. The primary reason for inflation's wider impact is the existence of a tax system designed with stable prices in mind. This paper offers a brief summary of the effects of inflation on the tax treatment of the firm, focusing on four important decisions the firm makes: the scale of investment; the method of finance; the durability of assets used in production; and the holding period of these assets.

There are a number of interesting and related issues which cannot be covered in a paper of this length. As I will be considering inflation that is both uniform and fully anticipated, questions concerning the behavior of the firm in response to uncertainty about inflation, or to a concommitant change in relative prices, will not arise.

I. The Model

Let us consider a simple model of a corporation which uses a single type of capital good in producing one type of output. The firm seeks to maximize the wealth of its shareholders, who discount after-tax cash flows at rate e and are subject to personal taxes on dividends at rate θ, and capital gains, at an accrual-equivalent rate c. The firm pays taxes at rate τ on corporate profits, which are calculated by deducting interest payments and depreciation allowances from gross cash flows. The nominal interest rate is i, and b is the fraction of capital structure that the firm chooses to devote to debt.

All capital goods are assumed to have service patterns which decline exponentially; the rate of decay δ is indicative of how durable the asset is. The price, relative to that of output sold concurrently, of a unit

of capital of type δ yielding a certain standard level of capital services is $q(\delta)$. All prices inflate at rate π. As the purpose of this paper is to focus on the specific impact of inflation, I shall consider the simple case in which depreciation allowances accorded assets would reflect actual economic depreciation in the absence of inflation, but which are based on historic cost. This implies that the nominal depreciation allowance received by an asset of age t and type δ is $\delta e^{-\delta t}$ times its original purchase price. I also omit the investment tax credit in the interest of simplicity.

Firms not only choose the durability of the assets used, but the length of time T that they are held before being sold and replaced. Upon such resale, firms are taxed at rate $\gamma \leqslant \tau$ on the difference between sale price and basis (the nominal value of remaining depreciation deductions).

As shown in the Appendix, the firm's optimal behavior may be viewed as a two-stage process. In the first stage, it chooses the decay rate δ, the holding period T, and the debt-value ratio b to minimize the "user cost" of capital, which is the shadow rental price of capital goods. In the second stage, the firm invests until the marginal product of capital goods equals this minimized cost. For given values of δ, T, and b, the user cost is

$$(1) \quad C = \frac{q(\delta)(\rho+\delta)}{(1-\tau)}\left[(1-\tau z)+(\gamma-\tau z)\right.$$

$$\left. \times (1-e^{-\pi T})\left(\frac{e^{-(\rho+\delta)T}}{1-e^{-(\rho+\delta)T}}\right)\right]$$

where

$$(2) \quad \rho = \frac{bi(1-\tau)(1-\theta)+(1-b)e}{b(1-\theta)+(1-b)(1-c)} - \pi$$

may be interpreted as the real after-tax cost of funds to the firm and

$$(3) \quad z = \int_0^\infty e^{-(\rho+\pi)t} \delta e^{-\delta t} dt = \frac{\delta}{\rho+\pi+\delta}$$

is the present value of depreciation allowances accruing to an initial investment of one dollar which is never resold (discounted at the nominal discount rate $\rho + \pi$ because allowances are in nominal terms). To get an intuitive sense of what ρ represents, note that when $b=1$, $\rho = i(1-\tau)-\pi$, the interest rate net of tax deductions and inflation; when $b=0$, $\rho = (e/1-c)-\pi$.

Equation (1) differs from the standard formula for user cost because it explicitly accounts for the tax treatment of the disposal of assets by resale. It reduces to the basic formula when $T = \infty$.

II. The Effects of Inflation

A. *Asset Holding Period*

In a more general model than that considered here, firms might find it optimal to sell and replace assets of a certain vintage, rather than use them until fully exhausted, even in a world without taxes. In the current model, all assets are identical in productive characteristics, so such behavior could have no real consequences.

However, the introduction of taxes may cause assets identical in productive characteristics to differ in another sense. If depreciation allowances are accelerated, an asset declines in value faster than would be dictated by its decline in productivity alone. This is because it is now really two "assets": one that produces capital services, and one that "produces" depreciation deductions, the second declining in value more rapidly than the first. However, if the asset is sold, under current *U.S.* law the depreciation allowances that remain are not transferred. Rather, the sale price is used as a new basis for depreciation deductions. Thus, if the depreciation schedule is accelerated, the asset transfer will increase the value of remaining deductions and generate an increase in the value of the asset. This is countered by the

fact that the seller must pay a tax at rate γ on the difference between sale price and basis (the nominal value of remaining depreciation allowances). The rate γ simply equals τ for equipment, but for structures is actually a weighted average of the ordinary corporate rate and the lower corporate capital gains rate; the ordinary rate is applied only to the amount by which the asset's basis falls short of that which would have obtained had straight-line tax depreciation been used. (This practice is technically referred to as the "recapture" of "excess" depreciation, though such a designation is rather inappropriate.) Imagining a firm selling the asset to itself, we can see that it must weigh the increased value of depreciation allowances against the tax liability incurred on transfer.

When there is economic depreciation of assets, as I have assumed in this analysis, such a distortion disappears; basis and sale price would be identical and turnover would have no real impact on the firm. However, inflation once again introduces the same divergence caused by accelerated depreciation. Historic cost depreciation implies that turnover provides a step-up in basis, generating both an increase in the value of future depreciation deductions and an immediate tax liability.

This effect is represented by the second term in brackets in the cost of capital expression in equation (1). This term increases or decreases with T according to whether the turnover tax γ is less than or greater than the present value of tax deductions. Since, for structures, γ is approximately equal to τ, currently .46, for small values of T, and approximately equal to the corporate capital gains rate, currently .28, for T large (because the fraction of sale price less basis "recaptured" declines over time), the optimal holding period T, with positive inflation, will be zero, infinite, or somewhere in between according to whether $z \geqslant 1$, $z \leqslant .28/.46$ or $1 > z > .28/.46$. The first condition is never met, and the second requires that $\delta < (\rho+\pi)x(.28/.18)$. For a nominal discount rate of .10, this critical value of δ is .156, much higher than the rate of depreciation for any general category of structures.

Since $\gamma \equiv \tau$ for equipment, an optimal holding period less than infinity never obtains. Thus, for most assets, inflation will encourage holding assets, despite their inflation-eroded depreciation allowances, rather than replacing them.

B. Debt-Equity Ratio

As the Modigliani-Miller theorem shows, the choice of debt-equity ratio is of no consequence in a taxless world under a variety of circumstances, and debt dominates equity with a corporate tax but no personal taxes. However, in reality, holders of debt and equity pay taxes, too, and because of the favorable tax treatment of capital gains, the personal tax rate on debt income is higher for any given individual than the tax on equity income. Thus, the choice between debt and equity depends on the relative magnitudes of the corporate tax rate, τ, the capital gains rate, c, and the personal tax rate, θ. As I discussed in an earlier paper (1979b), the debt-equity choice is knife-edged if all investors possess the same tax rates, even in the presence of short sale constraints on individuals. However, with progressive taxes, an interior solution is possible in which firms are indifferent between debt and equity and individuals are specialized in clienteles.

To examine the effect of inflation on the debt-equity decision, I rewrite equation (2) by replacing i and e with the real, after-tax returns to holders of equity and debt, $e_N = e - \pi$, and $i_N = i(1-\theta') - \pi$, where θ' is the personal tax rate of those who hold debt, and not necessarily equal to θ. Equation (2) becomes

(4) $\quad \rho = [b(1-\theta) + (1-b)(1-c)]^{-1}$

$$\times \left\{ \left[bi_N(1-\tau)\left(\frac{1-\theta}{1-\theta'}\right) + (1-b)e_N \right] \right.$$

$$\left. + \pi \left[b\left(\frac{1-\theta}{1-\theta'}\right)(\theta'-\tau) + (1-b)c \right] \right\}$$

For given underlying real rates of return e_N and i_N, inflation influences the real cost of funds ρ in three ways, depicted in the term multiplying π in (4). First, corporations can deduct at rate τ the inflation premium component of the nominal interest rate; second, bondholders must pay tax rate θ' on the same amount. Thus, for i_N given, debt becomes cheaper to the firm as inflation increases if $\tau > \theta'$, and more expensive if $\tau < \theta'$. Although τ is directly observable, θ' is not, because individual tax rates differ; estimates of θ' vary considerably. From a comparison of returns on tax-exempt and taxable long-term debt, Roger Gordon and Burton Malkiel estimate θ' to have been approximately 22.5 percent in 1978. Using flow of funds data to identify holders of debt and calculate θ' directly, Martin Feldstein and Lawrence Summers arrive at a value of 42 percent for 1977. It is thus unclear to what extent inflation reduces the effective tax rate on debt, if at all, though it seems likely that no appreciable additional tax burden is introduced.

The final influence of inflation on ρ is through the taxation of nominal rather than real capital gains. Here, there is no question about the direction of the effect; for e_N given, equity becomes more expensive. Estimates of c, like those of θ', are not very accurate, though c may very well be under 10 percent, as suggested by Martin Bailey. (Remember that c is the accrual-equivalent of the tax rate on realizations.) Thus, for given values of e_N and i_N, the likely effect of inflation is to make debt a cheaper source of finance, and equity more expensive, encouraging greater use of the former. Of course, the general equilibrium effect of inflation on b is more complicated, for it must also depend on the behavior of e_N and i_N.

C. Choice of Asset Life

Assuming the choice of asset durability to be among values of δ in the "normal" range where the optimal holding period T is infinite, the cost of capital for given b and δ may be written more simply as

(5) $\quad C = \dfrac{q(\delta)(\rho + \delta)}{(1-\tau)}(1-\tau z)$

$$= q(\delta)\left[\frac{\rho}{1-\tau} + \delta + \frac{\tau\pi z}{1-\tau}\right]$$

Expression (5) shows that the user cost per dollar of capital consists of three terms: the gross of tax real firm discount rate, the rate of asset decay, and the rate of decline due to inflation in the value of the nominally denominated "asset" representing the present value of the stream of depreciation allowances.

Perhaps a commonly held belief is that this "inflation tax" on depreciation allowances weighs more heavily on longer-lived assets which have to wait longer to collect their depreciation allowances. This view is incorrect (see my 1979a article). For any given value of ρ, the required internal rate of return before taxes on an asset of type δ is

$$(6) \quad v(\delta) = \frac{C(\delta)}{q(\delta)} - \delta = (\rho + \tau\pi z)/(1-\tau)$$

It is evident that while inflation raises this rate for all values of δ, the rate of change increases monotonically with δ; the size of the inflation tax declines with asset durability.

It is important to realize that just as the increase in the tax burden on equity relative to debt does not *necessarily* imply that inflation will lead to increased leverage in a full general equilibrium model, the heavier rate of tax on short-lived assets needn't imply that a smaller value of δ will result from inflation. The ultimate answer depends on the behavior of the real after-tax return ρ. If ρ is fixed, there are two offsetting effects which determine the optimal δ. The relatively higher tax rate on short-lived assets will favor the choice of a small value of δ. However, the general increase in àll tax rates, with the resulting higher before-tax rate of return, favors the choice of short-lived assets with large values of δ. As has been pointed out by Richard Kopcke, the total effect on the choice of δ is ambiguous, as can be seen from considering the effect of π on the cost of capital. On the other hand, if ρ decreases with the increase in inflation, as Patric Hendershott has suggested, this

second effect favoring short-lived investment is lessened.

D. *Investment Scale*

The scale of investment depends on the cost of capital. If we hold constant the underlying rates of return to investors, e_N and i_N, and the other decision variables of the firm, b, δ and T, then the likely effect of inflation, as discussed by Feldstein and Summers, will be an increase in user cost and a drag on investment. The effect on ρ will be ambiguous but small relative to the increase in the inflation tax on depreciation allowances. For example, for representative values of the relevant parameters ($\theta = .4$, $\theta' = .3$, $\tau = .46$, $c = .1$, $T = \infty$, $b = .3$, $\delta = .1$, $\rho = .04$, and $\pi = .06$) an increase in the rate of inflation of $\Delta\pi$ raises ρ by $.036\Delta\pi$, while $\tau\pi z$ increases by $.161\Delta\pi$.

However two important qualifications are necessary. First, if the real after-tax rates of return e_N and i_N fall as a result of inflation, as some theory and evidence suggests, ρ will increase less (or decrease more) and so will user cost, than has been proposed. Moreover, to the extent that firms can alter their debt-equity ratio and choice of asset durability, this must also diminish the increase in user cost. The answer to how inflation affects the scale of investment thus depends in part on a number of empirical magnitudes about which more information should be acquired.

APPENDIX: THE FIRM'S OPTIMIZING BEHAVIOR

Let us assume the firm produces output with the concave production function $F(K)$, where K is the capital stock on hand. The firm seeks to maximize the wealth of its owners as represented by the present value of net cash flows, discounted at the equity rate e. As demonstrated in my earlier paper (1979b), this is equivalent to choosing b to minimize ρ (as presented in equation (2) in the text), and then maximizing the present value, calculated with discount rate $\rho + \pi$, of flows to the firm before interest payments

and debt issues. Letting I_t be the physical investment in capital at time t, this present value is

$$(A1) \quad v = \int_0^\infty e^{-(\rho+\pi)t}$$

$$\times \ (1-\tau)e^{\pi t}F\left(\int_{-\infty}^t I_s e^{-\delta(t-s)}ds\right)$$

$$-e^{\pi t}q(\delta)I_t(1-x)\bigg]dt$$

where x is the present value of depreciation allowances times τ plus turnover tax payments per dollar of investment. If each asset is turned over every T years, the present value of depreciation deductions it receives per initial dollar is

$$(A2) \quad \int_0^T e^{-(\rho+\pi)t}\delta e^{-\delta t}dt$$

$$+e^{-\rho T}\int_T^{2T}e^{-(\rho+\pi)(t-T)}\delta e^{-\delta t}dt+\dots$$

$$=z\left(\frac{1-e^{-(\rho+\pi+\delta)T}}{1-e^{-(\rho+\delta)T}}\right)$$

which exceeds z because of the step-up in basis every T years. The present value of turnover tax payments is

$$(A3) \quad \gamma\bigg[e^{-\rho T}e^{-\delta T}(1-e^{-\pi T})$$

$$+e^{-2\rho T}e^{-2\delta T}(1-e^{-\pi T})+\dots\bigg]$$

$$=\gamma\left(\frac{e^{-(\rho+\delta)T}}{1-e^{-(\rho+\delta)T}}\right)(1-e^{-\pi T})$$

Combining (A2) and (A3) yields

$$(A4) \quad x=\tau z+(\tau z-\gamma)$$

$$\times(1-e^{-\pi T})\left(\frac{e^{-(\rho+\delta)T}}{1-e^{-(\rho+\delta)T}}\right)$$

Insertion of this value of x into (A1) and differentiating v with respect to I_t yields the requirement that the marginal product of capital F' equals C, as represented in equation (1) in the text. Differentiation of v with respect to δ and T yields the conditions that $\partial c/\partial\delta$ and $\partial C/\partial T$ should equal zero.

REFERENCES

A. J. Auerbach, "Inflation and the Choice of Asset Life," *J. Polit. Econ.*, June 1979, *87*, 621–38.

———, "Wealth Maximization and the Cost of Capital," *Quart. J. Econ*, Aug. 1979, *93*, 434–46.

M. J. Bailey, "Capital gains and Income Taxation," in Arnold C. Harberger and Martin J. Bailey, eds., *The Taxation of Income from Capital*, Washington 1969, 11–49.

M. Feldstein and L. Summers, "Inflation and the Taxation of Capital Income in the Corporate Sector," *Nat. Tax. J.*, Dec. 1979, *32*, 445–470.

R. H. Gordon and B. G. Malkiel, "Taxation and Corporation Finance," memo. no. 31, Princeton Univ. Financial Research Center 1980.

P. H. Hendershott, "The Decline in Aggregate Share Values: Inflation, Taxation, Risk and Profitability," paper presented at Nat. Bur. Econ. Res. Conference on Taxation, Nov. 1979.

R. W. Kopcke, "Inflation, Corporate Income Taxation, and the Demand for Capital Assets," *J. Polit. Econ.*, forthcoming.

7

Inflation and the Choice of Asset Life

I. Introduction

One of the most important aspects of the one-sector monetary growth model developed by Tobin (1965) is the analysis of the effect of inflation on the steady-state capital intensity and real interest rate. Tobin showed that, by lowering the real return on money, inflation makes real capital more attractive as an asset and leads to capital deepening and a lower real rate of return. By including personal and corporate income taxes in the specification of this model, Feldstein (1976) has found that the failure to index these taxes for inflation may also have a substantial impact on the economy's steady-state characteristics. One aspect of the problem which has not been adequately explored is the effect of inflation on the production decisions of firms.

The current structure of the U.S. corporate income tax has the effect of greatly distorting investment decisions among various assets. The investment tax credit may be applied to purchases of certain equipment, but not structures. Even in the absence of inflation, de-

The author would like to thank Martin Feldstein for helpful discussions on this subject.

preciation schedules used for tax purposes do not mirror true economic depreciation.[1] With the advent of inflation, this distortion is compounded by the fact that these schedules are based on the original or "historic" cost and not the replacement cost of the capital being depreciated.[2]

In the next section, we present a model of competitive firm behavior when the durability of capital is subject to choice by the firm. A steady-state growth path will have two important characteristics when there is no corporate taxation. First, firms will evaluate capital investments of differing durability using the same discount rate. Second, the market value of a firm will exactly equal the reproduction cost of the capital assets which it owns.

The results are extended in Section III to the case where there is a corporate income tax. In the presence of inflation, the taxation of corporate profits may influence both the choice of asset life and the market value of corporate equity. It turns out that market value will equal reproduction cost if the tax schedule for asset depreciation corresponds to true economic depreciation, measured at replacement cost. The effective tax rate on corporate income will be independent of the choice of asset life if the depreciation schedule is a linear combination of such "replacement cost depreciation" and immediate expensing. When depreciation allowances mirror capital decay, but are not indexed for inflation, share value is depressed, and the choice of asset life is biased toward greater durability.

In Section IV, we integrate our analysis of the firm with the traditional one-sector monetary growth model. We derive in Section V the effect of inflation on the characteristics of the steady state. For the case in which depreciation allowances are properly indexed, an increase in the inflation rate leads to an increase in capital durability. The ability of firms to vary asset life causes greater capital deepening, and a smaller decline in the real rate of return, than occur in earlier models from an increase in inflation. Additional analytical results, supported by findings from a numerical simulation in Section VI, indicate that the failure to index depreciation allowances may induce a further shift to the use of more durable assets under inflationary circumstances.

II. The Choice of Asset Life

We consider first the question of optimal firm behavior in an economy with one production sector composed of competitive firms which

---

[1] See Samuelson (1964) for a discussion of tax deductibility and economic depreciation.

[2] Tideman and Tucker (1976) provide a detailed analysis on this subject.

utilize two inputs, capital and homogeneous labor, subject to constant returns to scale in production. The price of new "capital" goods at time t is, of course, equal to the price of all "other" goods, denoted p_t. The wage rate is w_t. The rate at which p and w inflate is denoted π. Savings by individuals may take the form of money or firm equity. The government issues money, which carries a fixed nominal return of zero, and raises the remainder of its required revenues through lump sum taxes and the taxation of corporate income.[3] The rate at which equity holders discount nominally measured flows from the firm is r.

Capital goods decay exponentially at a constant rate, δ. However, δ is variable ex ante and subject to choice by the firm. We assume that increases in δ increase the flow of capital services per unit of time from a unit of capital, such increases being subject to diminishing returns. This flow is represented by the function $A(\delta)$ ($A' > 0$, $A'' < 0$). Gross output is defined by

$$Y^G = H(KS, L); \quad H_K, H_L, H_{KL} > 0; \quad H_{KK}, H_{LL} < 0, \qquad (1)$$

where H is homogeneous of degree one in its two inputs, labor, L, and capital services, KS. Let I_t be the nominal investment at time t, and δ_t the corresponding decay rate chosen by the firm. Then, the net capital stock remaining from this investment at time $s > t$ is $(I_t/p_t)e^{-\delta_t(s-t)}$. Thus, total capital services at time s are

$$KS_s = \int_{-\infty}^{s} A(\delta_t)(I_t/p_t)e^{-\delta_t(s-t)}dt. \qquad (2)$$

Corporate profits are taxed at rate τ, after the deduction of wages and depreciation allowances. We denote as $D(x, \delta)$ the deduction permitted per dollar of initial investment for an asset of age x which decays at rate δ.

In the model we are considering, with no uncertainty or market imperfections, the firm's objective is the maximization of the current wealth of shareholders through the maximization of its own present value, which is

$$V = \int_{0}^{\infty} e^{-rt} [(1-\tau)(p_t Y_t^G - w_t L_t) - I_t + \tau \int_{-\infty}^{t} I_s D(t-s, \delta_s)ds]dt. \qquad (3)$$

[3] We thus do not consider the corporate financing decision between debt and equity, and the interaction of corporate and personal capital income taxes on this decision, under inflationary conditions. Such a study is quite complex in itself and beyond the scope of this paper. Nevertheless, it is unlikely that a more elaborate model would yield results very different from those presented here. See the discussion at the end of Sec. V.

Differentiating V with respect to δ_t, I_t, and L_t, we obtain the first-order conditions for present value maximization. For all t,

$$\int_t^\infty [A'(\delta_t) - A(\delta_t)(s-t)]H_K(KS_s, L_s)e^{-(\rho + \delta_t)(s-t)}ds$$

$$= \frac{\partial}{\partial \delta_t}\{[1 - \tau z(\delta_t)]/(1-\tau)\}, \tag{4a}$$

$$\int_t^\infty A(\delta_t)H_K(KS_s, L_s)e^{-(\rho+\delta_t)(s-t)}ds = [1 - \tau z(\delta_t)]/(1-\tau), \tag{4b}$$

and

$$H_L(KS_t, L_t) = w_t/p_t, \tag{4c}$$

where $\rho = r - \pi$ is the real discount rate and

$$z(\delta) = \int_0^\infty e^{-rs}D(s, \delta)ds \tag{5}$$

is the present value of depreciation allowances for a unit of new capital which decays at rate δ.

Conditions (4a)–(4c) will always hold for the optimizing firm but may be greatly simplified for the special case of interest in this paper, the steady state. Let a unit of "effective capital" be that amount of capital which is needed to provide one unit of capital services per unit time. The size of a unit of effective capital is $[A(\delta)]^{-1}$, where δ is the decay rate of the capital in question. Similarly, the price of a new unit at time t is

$$p_t^* = p_t/A(\delta). \tag{6}$$

In a steady state, the value of δ chosen by firms will be constant over time. Thus, if we define the net capital stock available at time t in output units,

$$K_t = \int_{-\infty}^t (I_s/p_s)e^{-\delta(t-s)}ds; \tag{7}$$

then capital services at time t are $KS_t = A(\delta)K_t$. Since conditions (4a) and (4b) must hold for all t, we may differentiate them with respect to t to obtain conditions which also must hold. Substituting these back into the original conditions and using (7), we rewrite the first-order conditions (4a)–(4c) (dropping time subscripts) as

$$\frac{\partial c}{\partial \delta} = 0, \tag{8a}$$

$$H_K[A(\delta)K, L] = c/p, \tag{8b}$$

and

$$H_L[A(\delta)K, L] = w/p, \tag{8c}$$

where

$$c_t = p_i^*(\rho + \delta)(1 - \tau z)/(1 - \tau) \tag{9}$$

is the shadow price of capital, measured in effective units, referred to by Jorgenson (1963) as the "user cost of capital." We may interpret the optimal steady-state production behavior of the firm, outlined in equation (8), as having two steps. In the first step, described by equation (8a), firms minimize the implicit cost of capital services, c, by their choice of δ. Once this is done, labor and capital services are combined to maximize profits, with their marginal revenue products being equated with their marginal costs.[4]

Swan (1970) has studied the problem of firms which perform the first of the productive steps described above, the creation of capital services through choice of δ, for the special case in which $\tau = 0$. In this situation, (8a) simplifies to

$$\rho + \delta = -\frac{p^*}{\partial p^*/\partial \delta}, \tag{10}$$

which is precisely the condition derived by Swan.

We next discuss the firm value which results in a steady state. Substituting (7), (8a)–(8c), and (9) into (3), we obtain

$$V = p_0 K_0 (1 - \tau z) + \tau \int_0^\infty e^{-rt} \int_{-\infty}^0 I_s D(t-s)ds \, dt. \tag{11}$$

Thus, the ratio of firm value to the reproduction cost of its net capital stock is

$$q = (1 - \tau z) + (p_0 K_0)^{-1}\tau \int_0^\infty e^{-rt} \int_{-\infty}^0 I_s D(t-s)ds \, dt.[5] \tag{12}$$

When there are no corporate taxes, $q = 1$, so that the market value of a firm equals the replacement cost of its tangible assets.

---

[4] Since we have assumed constant returns to scale in production, eqq. (8a)–(8c) define only the optimal ratio between capital services and labor and not the level of each. Further, (8b) and (8c) may be solved independently for this ratio and must give the same value in equilibrium.

[5] Note that q differs from the marginal increase in firm value resulting from an additional dollar of investment. It is easily verified that, at an optimum, the latter must always equal unity. In the language of Tobin and Brainard (1977), we are measuring the average and not the marginal value of q.

III. Taxation and Depreciation

With the advent of corporate taxation, firm behavior changes due to changes in the capital rental price, c. If we define the firm's "implicit discount rate" to be

$$\nu = (\rho+\delta)(1-\tau z)/(1-\tau) - \delta, \tag{13}$$

then it is easily verified that firms behave exactly as they would in a world without taxation, using ν rather than ρ as the relevant discount rate. Since investors still receive a rate of return equal to ρ, the effective corporate tax rate may be defined as

$$\theta = (\nu-\rho)/\nu. \tag{14}$$

Of course, if $\tau = 0$, then $\nu = \rho$ and $\theta = 0$. When $\tau > 0$, the magnitude of θ depends on the depreciation scheme followed. Further, θ may vary according to the rate of capital decay chosen.

Suppose that the actual tax laws allowed a fraction e of all capital to be expensed,[6] with the remaining capital allowed true economic depreciation, measured at current replacement cost. The value of z for expensed capital is one, since the full deduction is received immediately. From a dollar of capital purchased at time t, the amount available at time s is $(1/p_t)e^{-\delta(s-t)}$. The value of such capital at current prices is found by multiplying this term by p_s. Multiplying the resulting term by δ gives the value of $D(s-t, \delta)$ for economic replacement cost depreciation:

$$D_R(s-t, \delta) = \delta e^{-\delta(s-t)}(p_s/p_t). \tag{15}$$

The present value of such allowances is

$$z_R = \delta/(\rho+\delta). \tag{16}$$

Thus, the total value of z per unit of capital would, in the case with a fraction e expensed, be

$$z_e = e + (1-e)\delta/(\rho+\delta). \tag{17}$$

Substitution into equation (13) gives

$$\nu = \rho(1-\tau e)/(1-\tau). \tag{18}$$

The effective tax rate is, therefore,

$$\theta = \tau(1-e)/(1-\tau e), \tag{19}$$

which is not dependent on δ. The effective tax rate varies from zero, when full expensing is followed, to τ, when $e = 0$.[7]

---

[6] I.e., deducted as a current expense upon purchase.

[7] Similar results have been derived by King (1975) and Harberger (1979) for the case in which $\pi = 0$.

Now, consider the case where depreciation allowances mirror true decay of capital but are measured at original or "historic" cost. The deduction allowances are

$$D_H(s-t, \delta) = \delta e^{-\delta(s-t)}. \tag{20}$$

The present value of such allowances is

$$z_H = \delta/(\rho + \pi + \delta). \tag{21}$$

Substitution into equation (13) yields

$$\nu = \rho/(1-\tau) + \pi\tau z_H/(1-\tau), \tag{22}$$

and, from equation (14),

$$\theta = (\tau\rho + \pi\tau z_H)/(\rho + \pi\tau z_H). \tag{23}$$

We may observe two things. First, if $\pi > 0$, θ is greater than τ, the value of the effective tax rate when the depreciation schedules are indexed [see eq. (19)]. This extra "tax" may be understood by viewing the stream of tax savings from depreciation deductions as coupon receipts from a nominally denominated asset. In the absence of inflation, this asset has present value $\tau z_H/(1-\tau)$, since the tax savings are not, themselves, subject to taxation. When the price level increases by π, the real value of this asset decreases, since it is not indexed, at rate π, which involves a real cost of $\pi\tau z_H/(1-\tau)$, which appears on the right-hand side of equation (22), along with the real, before-tax cost of funds, $\rho/(1-\tau)$. Of equal importance is the fact that the size of this "depreciation asset," and hence its annual loss in value due to inflation, increases with δ. Thus, $d\theta/d\delta > 0$, and the choice of asset durability is biased toward the choice of long-lived assets with low values of δ.

We now consider the effect of corporate taxation on the value of q, the ratio of a firm's market value to the reproduction cost of its capital stock.

When replacement cost economic depreciation is allowed, the value of q is

$$q_R = (1-\tau z_R) + (p_0 K_0)^{-1}\tau \int_0^\infty e^{-rt} \int_{-\infty}^0 (I_s/p_s)p_t\delta e^{-\delta(t-s)}ds \, dt, \tag{24}$$

which, using equation (7), yields

$$q_R = (1-\tau z_R) + (p_0 K_0)^{-1}\tau p_0 K_0 z_R = 1. \tag{25}$$

The equality between capital reproduction cost and firm value is maintained.

When firms are permitted to expense purchases of capital immedi-

ately, $z = 1$, and the second term on the right-hand side of equation (12) disappears, since no capital currently owned by the firm has any depreciation allowances remaining. Thus, $q = 1 - \tau$. For a scheme in which firms may expense a fraction e of new purchases, following replacement cost depreciation for the rest, the value of q is

$$q_e = e(1-\tau) + (1-e) = 1-\tau e. \tag{26}$$

When allowances are not indexed but otherwise reflect economic depreciation, q drops below unity with the advent of inflation. The precise value of q depends on the age structure of a unit of a firm's capital stock. The older a unit of capital is, the lower the price level at which its depreciation allowances are computed. This makes older capital less desirable than new capital, which has a price per unit of p_t at time t. Thus, the average valuation per unit of firm-held capital must be lower than p_t and will decline as the average age of the net capital stock increases.

In a steady state, a representative firm increases its real investment at each moment in time at rate n, the growth of the labor force in the economy. Thus, the firm investment flows at times t and s are related by

$$(I_t/p_t) = (I_s/p_s)e^{-n(s-t)}. \tag{27}$$

Therefore, the net capital stock at time s is

$$K_s = \int_{-\infty}^{s} (I_s/p_s)e^{-n(s-t)}e^{-\delta(s-t)}dt = (I_s/p_s)/(n+\delta). \tag{28}$$

For the case of historic cost depreciation, we may use equations (20), (21), and (27) to express q as

$$q_H = 1-\tau z_H + (p_0 K_0)^{-1}\tau \int_0^{\infty} e^{-rt} \int_{-\infty}^{0} (I_0/p_0)e^{ns}p_s\delta e^{-\delta(t-s)}ds\, dt. \tag{29}$$

Equation (29) may be simplified with the aid of (28) to yield

$$q_H = (1-\tau z_H) + \tau z_H[1-\pi/(n+\delta+\pi)] = 1-\tau z_H\pi/(n+\delta+\pi), \tag{30}$$

which confirms that $q < 1$, for $\pi > 0$, and that q decreases as n decreases, since the average age of the firm's capital stock increases.

Thus, even if depreciation allowances do reflect economic depreciation appropriately, the failure to index such allowances influences corporate activity in two important ways. First, the effective corporate tax rate becomes related systematically to the durability of capital used in production, with a higher rate being assessed on short-lived assets. Second, the market value of a representative corporation drops below the replacement value of its capital stock. These two results will, in turn, influence the characteristics of the steady-state growth path of the economy.

IV. Steady-State Behavior

In this section, we incorporate the foregoing analysis of the firm into a neoclassical growth model. A complete presentation of the basic model may be found in Solow (1970).

In a steady state, gross output may be expressed as a function of the capital stock, labor in use, and capital decay rate:

$$Y^G = G(K, L, \delta) = H[A(\delta)K, L].\tag{31}$$

The corresponding value of net output is Y^G less capital decay:

$$Y^N = F(K, L, \delta) = G(K, L, \delta) - \delta K.\tag{32}$$

Since the functions G and F are homogeneous of degree one in K and L, we may divide by L to write each in intensive form:

$$y^G = g(k, \delta) = h[A(\delta)k]\tag{33}$$

and

$$y^N = f(k, \delta) = g(k, \delta) - \delta k.\tag{34}$$

Using equations (13) and (34), we may rewrite the first-order conditions for firm optimization, equations (8a)–(8c), more conveniently as

$$f_\delta = k \frac{\partial v}{\partial \delta},\tag{35a}$$

$$f_k = v,\tag{35b}$$

and

$$f = vk + \frac{w}{p}.\tag{35c}$$

We assume that the economy has a population growing at rate n, with labor supplied inelastically,[8] and that government expenditures comprise a fixed fraction, γ, of net output. These expenditures are financed, in part, by expanding the money supply at a nominal growth rate, g. The rest of the required revenue is raised through taxes, including the corporate income tax. Letting m and T represent real money balances and taxes per capita, the government budget constraint is

$$\gamma f(k, \delta) = gm + T.\tag{36}$$

Disposable income is defined to be gross income, less taxes and capital losses in the value of money and equity holdings. Money balances

---

[8] When Harrod-neutral technical change is present, n is interpreted as the population growth rate plus the rate of innovation.

decline in value at the rate of inflation, so that the per capita loss on money balances is

$$\Delta_m = \pi m. \tag{37}$$

Per capita losses in the value of equity could be calculated directly. However, there is a much simpler way. Since the net capital stock must grow at rate n, gross investment must satisfy

$$I_t/p_t = (n+\delta)K_t. \tag{38}$$

After accounting for new investment, the real value of equity in the economy must also grow at rate n:

$$(V_t/\dot{p}_t) = n(V_t/p_t) = nqK_t. \tag{39}$$

Since new investments raise firm value by the exact amount of their cost, the drop in value of current equity holdings, in per capita terms, must therefore be

$$\Delta_k = (n+\delta)k - nqk = [\delta + (1-q)n]k. \tag{40}$$

Disposable income as defined above is

$$y^d = g(k, \delta) - T - \Delta_m - \Delta_k. \tag{41}$$

In a steady state, real money balances must grow at rate n. Thus, $g - \pi = n$, and we may substitute equations (36), (37), and (40) into (41) to obtain

$$y^d = (1-\gamma)f(k, \delta) + nm - n(1-q)k. \tag{42}$$

Note that when there are no corporate taxes, or when depreciation allowances mirror true capital decay valued at current prices, the last term in equation (42) drops out.

At any time, real private wealth, representing equity and money balances, must grow at rate n. Let σ be the fraction of disposable income saved, that is, allotted to increases in wealth. Then,

$$\sigma y^d = n(m+qk). \tag{43}$$

The fraction of their portfolios which individuals seek to hold in real money balances is denoted $l/(1 + l)$. Therefore,

$$m = lqk. \tag{44}$$

From equations (42)–(44), we get

$$f(k, \delta)/k = \left[\frac{n(1+l)(1-\sigma)}{\sigma(1-\gamma)}\right]q + \left(\frac{n}{1-\gamma}\right) = aq + b. \tag{45}$$

In general, σ may be sensitive to the real rate of return, ρ, and l would

be expected to depend negatively on both ρ and π.[9] Thus, a is a function of ρ and π. By the assumptions stated above, b is fixed.

Since all gross output is either invested, consumed by the government, or consumed by the private sector, total private and public consumption per capita is:

$$C = g(k, \delta) - (n+\delta)k = f(k, \delta) - nk. \tag{46}$$

For any particular assumption about the structure of depreciation allowances, equations (12), (13), (35a)–(35c), (45), and (46) comprise a system of seven equations in eight unknowns: k, ρ, ν, w/p, δ, q, C, and π. By dropping (35c) and substituting (13) into (35a) and (35b), we obtain a system in k, ρ, δ, q, C, and π. By differentiating this system with respect to π, we may assess the impact that a change in the rate of inflation has on the steady-state values of the other five unknown variables.

V. The Effect of Changes in π

We first consider the case in which the depreciation schedule is a combination of expensing and replacement cost economic depreciation. Under this regime, the system defined at the end of the previous section reduces to

$$f_k = \rho(1-\tau e)/(1-\tau), \tag{47a}$$

$$f_\delta = 0, \tag{47b}$$

$$f/k = aq + b, \tag{47c}$$

$$q = 1 - \tau e, \tag{47d}$$

and

$$C = f - nk. \tag{47e}$$

Totally differentiating this system with respect to π, we obtain

$$\frac{dk}{d\pi} = a_\pi \cdot \Delta_1^{-1}, \tag{48a}$$

$$\frac{d\rho}{d\pi} = \Delta_0 \cdot \frac{dk}{d\pi}, \tag{48b}$$

[9] Some growth models assume optimizing behavior by households with infinite horizons (e.g., Sidrauski 1967). Under such conditions, savings must adjust to keep the steady-state value of ρ equal to the discount rate used by individuals in evaluating the utility of future consumption, so that a in eq. (45) is infinitely elastic with respect to ρ. The effect of changes in π in such a model may be found by dropping eqq. (47a) and (53a) in the following section and totally differentiating the remaining systems of equations for ρ fixed.

$$\frac{d\delta}{d\pi} = -\frac{f_{\delta k}}{f_{\delta\delta}} \cdot \frac{dk}{d\pi}, \qquad (48c)$$

$$\frac{dC}{d\pi} = (f_k - n)\frac{dk}{d\pi}, \qquad (48d)$$

and

$$\frac{dq}{d\pi} = 0, \qquad (48e)$$

where

$$\Delta_0 = \frac{(1-\tau)}{q} \cdot \left(\frac{f_{kk}f_{\delta\delta} - f_{k\delta}^2}{f_{\delta\delta}}\right) \qquad (49a)$$

and

$$\Delta_1 = \frac{kf_k - f}{qk^2} - a_\rho\Delta_0. \qquad (49b)$$

The first thing to notice about equations $(48a)$–$(48e)$ is that if the liquidity preference function, l (and hence a), is not dependent on π, then the system is insulated completely from the rate of inflation. In general, as long as $l_\pi \leq 0$ and $l_\rho \leq 0 \leq \sigma_\rho$, a_π and a_ρ are both less than or equal to zero.

By the definition of the net output, we have

$$f_{kk} = h''A^2, \qquad (50a)$$

$$f_{\delta\delta} = h''(kA')^2 + h'kA'', \qquad (50b)$$

and

$$f_{\delta k} = h''AA'k + f_\delta/k. \qquad (50c)$$

In the present case, $f_\delta = 0$, so that $f_{kk}, f_{\delta\delta}$, and $f_{\delta k}$ are all negative and

$$f_{kk}f_{\delta\delta} - f_{k\delta}^2 = h''h'kA^2A'' \qquad (51)$$

is positive. Thus, $\Delta_0 < 0$. Since the term $(kf_k - f)$ equals $[(Ak)h' - h]$, it is negative by the assumption that h is concave. It follows that $\Delta_1 < 0$. Therefore, $dk/d\pi > 0$, $d\rho/d\pi < 0$, and $d\delta/d\pi < 0$. Per capita consumption, C, increases with the increase in the capital-labor ratio if $f_k > n$, which is the condition that holds when k is below the value which would yield a "golden rule" growth path on which C would be at a maximum.[10]

As in earlier models in which the choice of asset life was not considered, inflation induces a desire on the part of individuals to shift their portfolio holdings from money to equity, and this leads to

[10] See Phelps 1961.

an increase in the capital-labor ratio and a decline in the real rate of return. Here, however, the capital deepening is accompanied by a shift to the use of more durable capital goods. As ρ declines, the user cost of capital [see eq. (9)] declines proportionally more for capital with small values of δ—durable capital. Firms alter their production behavior to take advantage of this tilting of relative prices.

The ability of firms to choose δ, with the resulting increase in asset durability, leads to a greater increase in k, and a smaller decrease in ρ, than would occur if δ were fixed. To demonstrate this, we first observe that if δ were fixed, then condition (47b) would no longer hold and would be replaced by the equation $\delta = \bar{\delta}$. Differentiating the new system with respect to π, we obtain

$$\frac{dk}{d\pi}\bigg|\delta = a_\pi \left[\frac{kf_k - f}{qk^2} - a_\rho \frac{(1-\tau)}{q} f_{kk} \right]^{-1} \qquad (52a)$$

and

$$\frac{d\rho}{d\pi}\bigg|\delta = \frac{(1-\tau)}{q} f_{kk} \cdot \frac{dk}{d\pi}, \qquad (52b)$$

so that Δ_0 has been replaced by $(1-\tau)f_{kk}/q$. It is easy to show that $\dfrac{dk}{d\pi} >$ $\dfrac{dk}{d\pi}\bigg|\delta$ and $\dfrac{d\rho}{d\pi} > \dfrac{d\rho}{d\pi}\bigg|\delta$. This result has a straightforward interpreta-

tion. As π increases, the induced increase in demand for equity increases k and drives down ρ until a new equilibrium is attained. For any given value of k which differs from the initial one, the ability to change δ means that a higher rate of return can be earned than in the case of constant δ. Thus, at the value of k that would obtain at a higher value of π with δ fixed, ρ would be higher and there would have to be an excess demand for equity. Therefore, the new equilibrium value of k must be higher when δ is not fixed, but not so high as to induce a drop in ρ to the value that would result with δ constant, since there would then be an excess supply of equity.

We now consider the case in which depreciation allowances follow actual economic depreciation but are not indexed. The relevant system of equations is

$$f_k = \rho/(1-\tau) + \tau\pi z_H/(1-\tau), \qquad (53a)$$

$$f_\delta = k\pi\left(\frac{\tau}{1-\tau}\right)(\rho+\pi)/(\rho+\pi+\delta)^2, \qquad (53b)$$

$$f/k = aq + b, \qquad (53c)$$

$$q = 1 - \tau \pi z_H / (n + \delta + \pi), \qquad (53d)$$

and

$$C = f - nk. \qquad (53e)$$

It is difficult to determine without ambiguity the effects of an increase in π beginning at positive rates of inflation.[11] For this purpose, we present a numerical simulation in the next section. We consider analytically the special case of a change in π starting at $\pi = 0$.

When $\pi = 0$, the steady state described by equations $(53a)$–$(53e)$ is identical with that described by equations $(47a)$–$(47e)$ when economic depreciation is followed ($e = 0$), so that we may assess the additional inflationary impact coming from the failure to index by comparing results derived from the two systems. Totally differentiating equations $(53a)$–$(53e)$, we obtain

$$\frac{dk}{d\pi} = (a_\pi - \tau z \Delta_4) \Delta_1^{-1}, \qquad (54a)$$

$$\frac{d\rho}{d\pi} = \Delta_0 \frac{dk}{d\pi} - \tau z \Delta_3, \qquad (54b)$$

$$\frac{d\delta}{d\pi} = - \frac{f_{\delta k}}{f_{\delta\delta}} \cdot \frac{dk}{d\pi} + k\left(\frac{\tau}{1-\tau}\right) \frac{\rho}{(\rho+\delta)^2} \cdot \frac{1}{f_{\delta\delta}}, \qquad (54c)$$

$$\frac{dC}{d\pi} = (f_k - n) \frac{dk}{d\pi}, \qquad (54d)$$

and

$$\frac{dq}{d\pi} = \frac{\tau z}{n+\delta}, \qquad (54e)$$

where Δ_0 and Δ_1 are as defined in $(49a)$ and $(49b)$ and

$$\Delta_3 = 1 - \frac{\rho k}{\delta(\rho+\delta)} \cdot \frac{f_{k\delta}}{f_{\delta\delta}} \qquad (55a)$$

and

$$\Delta_4 = \frac{a}{n+\delta} + a_\rho \Delta_3. \qquad (55b)$$

As discussed in Section III, the onset of inflation causes q to drop below unity because older units of capital have depreciation allowances which are smaller, in real terms, than those given for new capital. Thus, the average market value of the capital stock must be

[11] The added complexity of the problem results from the introduction of several effects not present above. Not only is the choice of δ now biased, but share price, q, and the rate of effective taxation, θ, are affected by a change in π. The net impact of these additional effects may be ambiguous under some conditions.

lower than if it were all new capital or if depreciation allowances were indexed.

The remainder of the results depends on the signs of Δ_3 and Δ_4. Clearly, Δ_3 is less than or equal to unity and may be negative. However, without knowing more about the production function, there is little more we can say. Using the definition of a, and the fact that $\Delta_3 \leq 1$, it follows that Δ_4 must be positive if

$$\eta_{\sigma\rho}/(1-\sigma) - l\eta_{l\rho}/(1+l) < \rho/(n+\delta), \qquad (56)$$

where $\eta_{\sigma\rho}$ and $\eta_{l\rho}$ are the elasticities of σ and l with respect to ρ. Since $l/(1+l)$ will be quite small relative to unity (see n. 13), condition (56) will hold unless the interest elasticity of savings is exceptionally high. For example, if we ignore the second term on the left-hand side of (56) and set $\sigma = .1, \rho = .06, n = .02$, and $\delta = .1$, the base values used in the following section's simulation, then (56) will hold as long as $\eta_{\sigma\rho} < .45$, a value which is higher than any empirical estimates of $\eta_{\sigma\rho}$ and much higher than most.

Therefore, assuming $\Delta_4 > 0$, the failure to index depreciation allowances leads initially to greater capital deepening resulting from inflation. This effect is due in part to the drop in q. Since the capital stock is "cheaper," the same amount of savings buys more of it. It is even more certain that the lack of replacement-cost depreciation leads to a greater shift to long-lived assets. Not only will the increase likely to occur in $dk/d\pi$ lead to this, but so will the heavier effective taxation of short-lived assets, which introduces a second term on the right-hand side of equation (54c). Since Δ_3 is of ambiguous sign, we cannot be sure of the additional impact on $d\rho/d\pi$.

We may summarize briefly the result of this section. If the demand for money is unresponsive to the rate of inflation, then proper indexing of depreciation allowances completely insulates the economy from inflation. When liquidity preference does depend on π, then $d\delta/d\pi < 0$. As in previous analyses, $dk/d\pi$ is positive and $d\rho/d\pi$, negative. However, the increase in k is larger and the decrease in ρ smaller than would be the case were the asset durability fixed.

When depreciation allowances are not indexed, the onset of inflation will likely lead to even more capital deepening and a greater shift to more durable capital, both because of the added increase in $dk/d\pi$, and because the "inflation tax" falls more heavily on short-lived assets. It is not clear whether these results will still hold at high levels of inflation. This question is explored in Section VI.

The introduction of corporate debt and personal income taxes to the present model would add realism but probably would not influence this section's results in an important way.

Consider first the indexed case, in which the effective tax rates on equity income and interest payments would not be affected by

inflation. Except for indirect portfolio effects caused by a decline in money holdings arising from an increase in π, we would not expect inflation to influence the equilibrium debt-equity ratio or the average tax rate on capital income in the corporate sector. Thus, we could interpret τ in equation (47) as this average tax rate, and our present results would be unaffected.

Without indexing, inflation would probably lead to a higher effective tax rate on equity returns, due to the taxation of nominal capital gains, but a lower effective tax rate on interest payments, since corporations may deduct nominal interest at a higher tax rate than individuals must generally pay on such income.[12] Thus, the effect of inflation on the average effective tax rate would depend on the degree to which a firm were initially levered and the shift induced in its debt-equity ratio. A massive movement toward debt could moderate the rise in the effective tax rate which results from the nonindexation of depreciation schedules. This result would reinforce our current findings, since a lower effective tax rate would yield a higher value of ρ for any given combination of k and δ, encouraging increased savings, a higher value of k, and [from eq. (54c)] a lower value of δ.

VI. An Example

Let gross output be governed by a modified Cobb-Douglas function:

$$g(k, \delta) = \phi k^\alpha \delta^\beta. \tag{57}$$

In our earlier terminology, $A(\delta) = \delta^{(\beta/\alpha)}$. The equilibrium conditions (53a)−(53e) become

$$\alpha\phi k^{\alpha-1}\delta^\beta - \delta = \rho/(1-\tau) + \pi\left(\frac{\tau}{1-\tau}\right)\delta/(\rho+\pi+\delta), \tag{58a}$$

$$\beta\phi k^{\alpha-1}\delta^{\beta-1} - 1 = \pi\left(\frac{\tau}{1-\tau}\right)(\rho+\pi)/(\rho+\pi+\delta)^2, \tag{58b}$$

$$\phi k^{\alpha-1}\delta^\beta - \delta = aq + b, \tag{58c}$$

and

$$q = 1 - \pi\tau\delta/[(\rho+\delta+\pi)(n+\delta+\pi)]. \tag{58d}$$

For simplicity, we consider the case in which a is fixed. Note that α is the gross capital share and will be larger than the share of capital in net production.

Reasonable values for the U.S. economy for the real growth rate, n, and the rate of corporate taxation, τ, are .02 and .4, respectively. Using values for γ and σ of $\frac{1}{3}$ and .1, and assuming l to be small

---

[12] See Feldstein, Green, and Sheshinski (1978) for a description of these effects.

TABLE 1

Simulation Results

π	q	δ	Half Life	ρ	f_k	k	g	C
.0	1.000	.100	6.93	.060	.100	25,000	10,000	7,000
.05	.941	.084	8.28	.051	.100	27,054	9,950	7,145
.10	.932	.074	9.35	.049	.104	27,230	9,683	7,121
.15	.935	.069	10.09	.049	.107	26,872	9,439	7,055
.20	.942	.065	10.60	.049	.109	26,461	9,252	6,992

relative to unity,[13] we may use equation (45) to calculate a and b, arriving at .27 and .03, respectively. We choose values for the production parameters ϕ, α, and β which, at $\pi = 0$, yield acceptable results for δ, the rate of capital decay, g, per capita output, and f_k, the net marginal product of capital. Christensen and Jorgenson (1969) have estimated δ for the period 1929–67 in the United States. Their estimates were .056 for nonresidential structures and .138 for producers' durables. We therefore choose .10 as the value for δ at $\pi = 0$. We also set f_k equal to .10, a value roughly in line with recent estimates by Feldstein and Summers (1977). We set per capita output at $10,000. The resulting values of the production parameters are

$$\phi = 112.47, \quad \alpha = .50, \text{ and } \beta = .25. \tag{59}$$

Table 1 presents simulation results for steady-state inflation values ranging between 0 and .2. Since capital decays exponentially, we include half-life as a measure of capital durability. Because $a_\pi = 0$ in this example, proper indexing means that π does not influence the system. Thus, the results in table 1 for $\pi = 0$ correspond to those for all values of π for the case in which replacement cost depreciation is allowed.

For low values of π, the results corroborate our previous findings: q declines, k increases, and δ declines. Because of the increase in k, C increases. The net marginal product of capital, f_k, is virtually unchanged, but ρ declines sharply because of the increase in θ due to the "inflation tax."

We can see that, once inflation reaches 10 percent, additional increases in π may not have the same effects. In particular, q begins to rise again and k falls, along with C. The marginal product of capital increases, so that ρ ceases to decline. However, the increase in capital durability continues, with asset life increasing an additional 13.4 percent between inflation rates of 10 and 20 percent.

[13] Feldstein (1976) has estimated the ratio in the United States of outside money to private wealth to be about 1 : 40.

One should be hesitant to draw firm conclusions from this simple example. However, it does illustrate the impact that the failure to index depreciation allowances can have on the choice of asset life, as well as other relevant economic variables.

VII. Conclusion

In this paper, we have introduced the choice of asset life into the neoclassical monetary growth framework and have explored how this choice may be influenced by the structure of depreciation allowances, particularly the fact that such allowances are generally not indexed to account for inflation. Our results, summarized in the introduction, should serve to emphasize the importance of this question.

References

Christensen, L. R., and Jorgenson, D. W. "The Measurement of U.S. Real Capital Input, 1929–1967." *Rev. Income and Wealth* 15 (December 1969): 293–320.
Feldstein, M. S. "Inflation, Taxes, and the Rate of Interest: A Theoretical Analysis." *A.E.R.* 66 (December 1976): 809–20.
Feldstein, M. S.; Green, J.; and Sheshinski, E. "Inflation and Taxes in a Growing Economy with Debt and Equity Finance." *J.P.E.* 86, no. 2, pt. 2 (April 1978): S52–S70.
Feldstein, M. S., and Summers, L. "Is the Rate of Profit Falling?" *Brookings Papers Econ. Activity* 1 (1977): 211–28.
Harberger, A. C. "Tax Neutrality in Investment Incentives." In *The Economics of Taxation,* edited by H. J. Aaron and M. J. Boskin. Washington: Brookings Inst., 1979, in press.
Jorgenson, D. W. "Capital Theory and Investment Behavior." *A.E.R.* 53 (May 1963): 247–59.
King, M. A. "Taxation, Corporate Financial Policy, and the Cost of Capital: A Comment." *J. Public Econ.* 4 (August 1975): 271–79.
Phelps, E. S. "The Golden Rule of Accumulation: A Fable for Growthmen." *A.E.R.* 51 (September 1961): 638–43.
Samuelson, P. A. "Tax Deductibility of Economic Depreciation to Insure Invariant Valuations." *J.P.E.* 72, no. 6 (December 1964): 604–6.
Sidrauski, M. "Rational Choice and Patterns of Economic Growth." *A.E.R.* 57 (May 1967): 534–44.
Solow, R. M. *Growth Theory: An Exposition.* Oxford: Oxford Univ. Press, 1970.
Swan, P. L. "Durability of Consumption Goods." *A.E.R.* 60 (December 1970): 884–94.
Tideman, T. N., and Tucker, D. P. "The Tax Treatment of Business Profits under Inflationary Conditions." In *Inflation and the Income Tax,* edited by H. Aaron. Washington: Brookings Inst., 1976.
Tobin, J. "Money and Economic Growth." *Econometrica* 33 (October 1965): 671–84.
Tobin, J., and Brainard, W. C. "Asset Markets and the Cost of Capital." In *Economic Progress, Private Values, and Public Policy: Essays in Honor of William Fellner,* edited by B. Balassa and R. Nelson. Amsterdam: North-Holland, 1977.

Index

T0329611